Prayers *for a* Woman's Heart

Elizabeth George

HARVEST HOUSE PUBLISHERS
EUGENE, OREGON

Cover by Dugan Design Group

Prayers for a Woman's Heart
Copyright © 2018 by Elizabeth George
Published by Harvest House Publishers
Eugene, Oregon 97408
www.harvesthousepublishers.com

ISBN 978-0-7369-7051-8 (pbk.)
ISBN 978-0-7369-7056-3 (eBook)

Library of Congress Cataloging-in-Publication Data

Names: George, Elizabeth, 1944- author.
Title: Prayers for a woman's heart / Elizabeth George.
Description: Eugene, Oregon : Harvest House Publishers, 2018.
Identifiers: LCCN 2017049209 (print) | LCCN 2017057862 (ebook) | ISBN 9780736970563 (ebook) | ISBN 9780736970518 (pbk.)
Subjects: LCSH: Christian women—Prayers and devotions.
Classification: LCC BV4844 (ebook) | LCC BV4844 .G4265 2018 (print) | DDC 242/.843—dc23
LC record available at https://lccn.loc.gov/2017049209

Printed in the United States of America

18 19 20 21 22 23 24 25 26 / BP-JC / 10 9 8 7 6 5 4 3 2 1

Contents

Introduction

I have called upon You,
for You will hear me, O God;
Incline Your ear to me, and hear my speech.

PSALM 17:6

If you stop and really think about it, prayer is a phenomenal privilege you have to communicate with the all-powerful God of the universe—who hears your prayers! Prayer is also an opportunity to bare your heart and pour out your soul to your loving heavenly Father—who cares deeply for you.

As you begin this book of prayers and inspiration to encourage you to keep coming before God, remember that in the Bible we are told countless times that we are to pray—to pray frequently, fervently, always, without ceasing, constantly, in and about everything. We are also told to pray purposefully—to pray according to the will of God because if we ask anything according to His will, He hears us" (1 John 5:14).

This book is not meant to teach you mechanics of prayer—the hows, the whens, the whys, and the whats—although I am praying it will be helpful to you as you draw closer to God. Instead it is meant to be used more like a devotional—a tool or a prompt for your own personal and private times of prayer.

God already knows your heart and your needs, and He wants to hear your prayers. He is available to listen to you for as long as you want to talk with Him, and as often as you desire to approach Him. And on those occasions when you want to pray but aren't sure what to say, His Holy Spirit will intercede on your behalf (Romans 8:26-27).

As a child of God, knowing Him and being able to talk with Him through prayer is your great privilege. Take advantage of this blessing often, and may this devotional book of prayers be a guide and a friend on your journey toward a life of prayer.

In His everlasting love,

Elizabeth George

Praise

God, before I place my feet on the floor
this morning—and every morning—
may I dedicate my day and myself to You.
Today I commit to bless and serve my family
and others You bring across my path.
And I will count it joy—all joy—to rely on
Your strength when trials come my way.
Praise Your holy name!

Amen.

If today is "one of those days" you would rather forget, remember that God is available to you every moment of it, no matter what you are facing. Choose not to focus on your problems, but to focus on God. Begin by praising Him for the gift of your salvation. A mere "Thank You" is hardly a sufficient response for the gifts of salvation and eternal life, but expressing continual praise to God will go a long way in showing your thankfulness.

So praise the Lord! Praise Him for the wonders that are at work in your life and in the lives of your loved ones. Proclaim His praise to the people you meet. Praising God is a wonderful way to testify to the reality of the living God. Praise Him for the true joy you find in Him and in His promises. Ask Him for grace—and thank and praise Him for it. Ask God to help you remember to go to Him for His comfort and guidance in your times of need.

Until you are with the Lord forevermore, there will always be suffering, disappointment, dashed dreams, and even ridicule and persecution. It is at these times you may not feel like praising God, but let your suffering cause you to offer to Him a sacrifice of praise. James 1:2-3 reminds you to "count it all joy when you fall into various trials, knowing that the testing of your faith produces patience." Praise God and His blessed Son with every step and every breath you take today.

By Him let us continually offer
the sacrifice of praise to God,
that is, the fruit of our lips,
giving thanks to His name.
HEBREWS 13:15

Help!

*Lord, I lay before You my worries, my sorrows,
my disappointments, and my failures.
I place before You my mountainous workload.
I am looking to You for a portion of Your strength
for today—and for joy in my work.
I am rejoicing in You, Lord—in my relationship
with You, Abba Father. I am presenting myself to You and
purposing, by Your grace, to set aside my thoughts of
hopelessness and helplessness—and panic—
and replace them with sure faith and trust in Your
presence and Your power. As I rise to take on the tasks
ahead of me, I give thanks as I remember that
"My help comes from the LORD."*

Amen.

Psalm 121 is one of the "Pilgrim Psalms" or "Songs of Ascent." Each year God's people were required to attend the annual festivals in Jerusalem. Fulfilling this law called for a commitment to a long and strenuous journey—an uphill climb every step of the way up to the mountaintop where the temple, the seat of worship, was located. These devoted worshippers trekked through desert lands where bandits often robbed the pilgrims along the way. Families banded together and traveled in caravans to provide safety for all family members, from babes to the aged. And they sang these songs as they ascended the terrain to the temple!

Many of our days are uphill climbs. Our climbs at home and at work often involve stress, weariness, and the challenge of managing heavy burdens and workloads. It's hard some days to find any joy as we labor on. Yet these pilgrims sang! They sang songs like Psalm 121 to praise God as they pushed themselves and their gear uphill. On their way to worship God, they worshipped Him with songs of praise. Through music they rehearsed God's promises as they struggled onward and upward. They recounted His character. And they recalled His faithfulness.

As you step into your day and step up to take on your responsibilities, with every step you take, lift up your eyes to the Lord. Lift up your songs of praise when you are worn out and weary. Lift up your heartfelt worship as you labor. Your help comes from the Lord.

> *I will lift up my eyes to the hills—*
> *from whence comes my help?*
> *My help comes from the LORD,*
> *who made heaven and earth.*
> *He will not allow your foot to be moved;*
> *He who keeps you will not slumber...*
> *neither slumber nor sleep.*

PSALM 121:1-4

Energy

*Father, today it feels as though
there's not much left of me. This morning
my energy level hit a wall, and in my own strength
I can go no further. But I praise You, God of all strength,
for when I am weak, You are strong. Thank You, Father,
that when my energy wanes, You quiet my heart and
bring comfort and peace of mind to my weary soul.
I love You, Lord. And I love the work I do—
the work that blesses my family and the people
You bring my way. Today I want to follow
Jesus' advice and "seek first the kingdom of God
and His righteousness" and all these things
shall be added to me (Matthew 6:33).*

Amen!

You have probably heard the saying, "A woman's work is never done," and you probably agree! It's as Solomon mused: "That which has been is what will be...there is nothing new under the sun" (Ecclesiastes 1:9). Day after day we are presented with another day of work. Work is definitely here to stay, but there are some practices and principles that can turn your workload into a wonder and your drudgery into something delightful.

- Meet with the Lord first thing every morning. As you pray, give Him your life, your heart, your day, and your work. Spend some time in His Word and absorb the most powerful energy available in the entire world—the energy only the Lord God can give you.

- Create a to-do list and a schedule for the day. What must be done...and when? Who needs what, and where, and when? Doing what matters gives you energy because it is rewarding. You know you are doing what's most important, so you have no guilt, no remorse, no dread.

- Learn and apply effective time management principles. Operate on a schedule. Use your calendar or phone app to keep track of appointments, events, commitments, lists, deadlines, and due dates.

- A little exercise makes a big difference. A walk or jog and a few exercises will rev you up right away and build you up for greater endurance.

The real key to easing your daily burdens is found in Isaiah 40:31. It begins with this focused principle for all believers:

Those who wait on the LORD shall renew their strength;
they shall mount up with wings like eagles,
they shall run and not be weary,
they shall walk and not faint.

Endurance

Dear God of all patience, You are longsuffering in
Your dealings with mankind…and with me.
You are not willing that any should perish,
and You patiently postpone Your judgment
so others may be brought to salvation.
Gracious Father, through Your dear Son, Jesus,
You have brought me Your priceless salvation
through His death on the cross.
Throughout the ages Your people have been
hated and persecuted. Grant me the strength
I need today and every day to persevere
as I count on the fulfillment of Your promise that
eternal salvation is awaiting me
at the end of my days on earth.

Amen.

It's amazing that people—including you and me—can endure just about anything if we believe it is for something worthwhile. Knowing that His disciples would be hated, arrested, and killed for following Him, Jesus made this promise: "He who endures to the end will be saved" (Matthew 10:22). Jesus' words and His promise still apply today. He promised salvation for all those who endure. Jesus was not saying that enduring suffering is a *way* to be saved, because endurance is not a means to earn salvation. No, endurance is the *evidence* that we are truly saved by Christ's death on our behalf.

You can praise God that He has not left you without His support as you faithfully persist through hard times. God has put His Spirit in you to help you endure whatever comes your way. He has made this promise to all believers: "I will make an everlasting covenant with them, that I will not turn away from doing them good" (Jeremiah 32:40).

When you are struggling, remember that the secret to endurance comes from your relationship with Jesus Christ, your Lord. As you trust in Him and are obedient to Him, the Holy Spirit who abides in you will empower you to stand firm against any and all trials and tribulation. Look to God daily and trust Him to give you His patience to endure every small or large test you face. Be patient and press on! Eternal life and peace in the presence of your Savior is your coming reward.

Perseverance is more than endurance.
It is endurance combined with
absolute assurance and certainty
that what we are looking for is going to happen.
OSWALD CHAMBERS

Confidence

*Dear God, Your very name Elohim
conveys that You stand for might, power, and
omnipotence as seen in the creation of the universe
and all that is in it, including me! No one can stand
before You in defiance. Every knee shall ultimately bow
before Your throne in utter submission. And yet,
that incredible power dwells in me through the presence
of Your Holy Spirit. Help me draw on Your strength and
power so I can run and not be weary, and I can walk
and not faint as I tap into Your empowering Spirit.
By Your grace, today I will confidently live for You
with strength and resolve, and by Your grace,
I will not shrink from fulfilling Your will,
for I can do all things through Christ
who strengthens me!*

Amen.

Self-confidence, self-reliance, and self-sufficiency are traits that are admired and desired by many women. Yet such self-sufficiency is an enemy to your soul, causing you to think you can always do what needs to be done in your own strength and with your own abilities. The man Gideon in the Old Testament could have possessed this kind of self-confidence when he prepared to meet his enemy with 32,000 men! But to prevent this kind of "self" attitude and "self" sufficiency God reduced Gideon's army down to a mere 300 men. With a force this small, there could be no doubt that any victory would be from God (see Judges 7:1-25). God wanted Gideon's confidence to be in Him—in Elohim and His might and power—and not his own abilities and resources.

Nothing has changed these thousands of years later. Like Gideon, you too must recognize the danger of trying to fight your battles in your own strength. God wants you to be victorious, but He wants you to know that any and all victory comes from Him, and He has given you the Holy Spirit to help you be victorious. Like Gideon, the apostle Paul recognized where his power came from: "My speech and my preaching were not with persuasive words of human wisdom, but in demonstration of the Spirit and of power" (1 Corinthians 2:4). God never sends you out to battle alone. He goes before you, as well as beside you and behind you. Whatever your situation, be confident. God, the mighty Elohim, is with you. *- Deut 31:8*

> *The angel of the LORD encamps*
> *all around those who fear Him,*
> *and delivers them.*
>
> PSALM 34:7

Anger

Righteous Father,
Your Word says to be angry and do not sin,
and to not let the sun go down on my wrath.
I acknowledge that most often my anger is
not a godly, righteous anger. It is a sinful display
of my utter need for Jesus' continued work in my life.
I ask that Your Holy Spirit work in me to help curb
my wrath and anger and to manifest Your love, patience,
and self-control. Then I will honor You as I live
according to Your standards and show the world
Your transforming grace in my life
through Jesus Christ.

Amen.

Is there such a thing as "good anger"? Yes, Jesus showed us an anger that was a holy response to sin when He was angry with the religious leaders for their uncaring attitudes toward a sick man (Mark 3:5). The Bible tells us that the right kind of anger is okay, but it points out that it is important to handle our anger quickly and not let it linger, giving the devil an opportunity for us to sin (Ephesians 4:26). Unfortunately, most of our anger is not righteous but results from pride, selfishness, and hurt feelings. When we don't get what we want, we get mad and sin by expressing our anger in harmful verbal and physical ways.

Anger is not anything new. The first son of Adam and Eve, Cain, was confronted by God for his anger. Why was Cain angry? Because God had no regard for his sacrifice, while his brother Abel's sacrifice was accepted. God told Cain that his anger was a "sin" which "lies at the door. And its desire is for you, but you should rule over it" (see Genesis 4:5-7). Rather than mastering his anger, Cain unleashed it and murdered his brother Abel.

How can we master the kind of anger that is sinful? Understand that no one is immune from anger, and anger is always "crouching at the door." Realize that anger cannot master you if it isn't there, so ask God for His help in not giving in to anger in the first place. And when anger does show its ugly head, acknowledge your anger to God and confess it as sin. Follow David's example: "I will confess my transgressions to the LORD...." Then accept God's forgiveness: "...and You forgave the iniquity of my sin" (Psalm 32:5).

If we cannot control our tempers,
what has grace done for us?
CHARLES SPURGEON

Contentment

*Dear God of all my provision, because of You,
I do not lack one good thing! You have provided me
with both physical and spiritual life. I acknowledge
and praise You that my everyday life and existence is
a gift to me from Your hand and Your heart.
You have promised that all I have and all I will ever
need will be provided by You in its proper time.
Lord, I thank You that I never need to worry about
what I will eat or drink or where I will lay my head
because You have also promised that as I seek
Your kingdom as my first priority, You will provide for
all my needs. Truly every good and perfect gift comes
down from You, and I shall not want for anything.*

Amen.

You need that car!" "You must have this new device!" How many times have you heard similar sales pitches? Our society is driven by discontentment, covetousness, and envy. James 4:2 describes our condition this way: "You lust and do not have. You murder and covet and cannot obtain." Like the apostle Paul advised, we should develop the opposite attitude: "I know how to be abased, and I know how to abound. Everywhere and in all things I have learned both to be full and to be hungry, both to abound and to suffer need" (Philippians 4:12).

Paul had to learn to be content, and maybe—just maybe—you do too. If you are having problems with being content, it helps to periodically readjust your perspective or reorder your priorities. It also helps to look to God's Word again and again and rely on His promises and Christ's power to help you be content. God promises to supply all you need—not all you want. How was Paul able to be content? Here's the answer in Paul's own words:

I have learned in whatever state I am, to be content:
I know how to be abased, and I know how to abound.
Everywhere and in all things
I have learned both to be full and to be hungry,
both to abound and to suffer need.
I can do all things through Christ who strengthens me.

PHILIPPIANS 4:11-13

Assurance

*Dear Jesus, in this world of daily uncertainties,
one thing is certain—eternal life! Long ago
You promised in Your Word that if I would
by faith believe in You as my Lord and Savior,
You would give me life everlasting.
Because of Your eternal power as the Son of God,
nothing and no one will ever be able to take me away
from You. Thank You, Lord Jesus, that I can live with
blessed assurance each day. May that confidence blossom
and grow as I trust You with the issues in my life.
My soul yearns for the day when I arrive in heaven
where I will bask in Your glory for all eternity.*

Amen.

When you accepted Jesus Christ as your Savior, you were promised and assured that you would have eternal life. What's also thrilling is that eternal life started the moment of your salvation. How can you nurture and strengthen this kind of assurance?

Look to God's Word. Understand that assurance is based on the Bible. The Bible is 100 percent true and trustworthy. You can believe what the Bible says because its message comes from God Himself (John 17:17).

Realize that a promise is only as valid as the one making the promise. Jesus Christ, God's Son, made a promise in John 10:27-28 that His sheep will hear His voice and follow Him, and He will give them eternal life. Neither God nor His Son has ever failed to fulfill His promises.

Rest in the assurance given through the resurrection of Jesus. Because of Jesus' death and resurrection, you, as His follower, need not fear death, for with His physical death comes eternal life (Romans 6:8). And because this assurance is based on Jesus' resurrection, you never have to worry about losing your salvation.

Relish and bask in the knowledge that as a believer you never have to wonder if you have done enough to merit salvation or fear that you have somehow forfeited your salvation. Your assurance in based in Jesus Christ, the Son of God and the perfect sacrifice for your sins. Today and every day, in Jesus Christ you are free to fellowship with God as you go about your daily activities. What joy! This assurance is worthy of your constant worship as you honor God with your every breath.

Assurance is the fruit that grows out of the root of faith.
STEPHEN CHARNOCK

Your Heart

O God, You are the searcher of all hearts!
I agree with Your Word that my heart is
sinful and desperately wicked. I want to do what is
right and good, but I confess that too often
I hurt others with my words, actions, and attitudes.
I know that these actions do not please You,
and I am humbly asking for Your forgiveness.
I am also asking You to search my heart and
see if there is anything that is keeping me from
obeying You and doing Your will.
By the power of Your Holy Spirit, may I serve
You, my family, and Your people
out of a pure heart of love.

Amen.

The Bible speaks of the "heart" and its actions almost 1,000 times! That indicates this topic is extremely important to God and should be to His people. Proverbs 4:23 strongly warns us to keep and guard our heart with all diligence, for "out of it spring the issues of life." The behavior we exhibit is the overflow of what's going on in our heart.

Because the heart is the control center of our emotions and actions, its watch-care cannot be a casual thing. The word "diligence" paints the picture of a guard who is on constant duty. No one but you can or should be assigned as the guardian of your heart. God is asking you to take full responsibility for the care of your heart—of your thoughts and actions.

Just as you have regular physical examinations, so you should regularly examine your heart. How is this done? Routinely read your Bible and pray. These two spiritual disciplines place you before God so He can work in Your heart. They allow the search-light of the Spirit to surface any areas in your life that need to be changed. Use the psalmist's words as a model for your own heartfelt prayer: "Search me, O God, and know my heart; try me, and know my anxieties; and see if there is any wicked way in me, and lead me in the way everlasting" (Psalm 139:23-24).

To have God speak to the heart
is a majestic experience, an experience that people may miss
if they monopolize the conversation and
never pause to hear God's responses.
CHARLES STANLEY

Helping or Hindering?

> God, You are the master builder and
> the chief architect of all of the beauty I see around me.
> From Your vantage point, You have orchestrated
> harmony and order in all Your creation, and Lord,
> You desire that same order and harmony for my life
> and family as well. It's so easy to hinder the atmosphere
> in my home and the health of my family relationships
> when I am selfish and stubborn. I know it's wrong, and
> I want to deal with these sins of selfishness and nagging.
> Help me to use my time, energy, and words to build up
> the family You have blessed me with.
>
> *Amen.*

Are you becoming a wife who is hindering rather than help-ing? If this is the direction of your life, then my fireplace story is a must! When Jim and I decided to do some remodeling in our little house, I was dead set on adding a fireplace. I knew we didn't have it in the budget, but I thought it should be, so I very cleverly made daily remarks like, "Wouldn't this be the perfect evening for a fire in the fireplace...if we had one?" Or, "Just think, if we had a fireplace, we could have dinner in front of a roaring fire." Finally, Jim said, "Elizabeth, are you helping or hindering?" Ouch!

Jim's words reminded me of the story in Ezra 5–6 about men who tried to hinder the rebuilding of God's temple, and how King Darius rebuked them and told them to stay away (Ezra 6:6-7). Unfortunately, it is all too easy to hinder positive progress.

Why not focus on being a woman who helps rather than hinders?

Follow the advice of Proverbs 14:1: "The wise woman builds her house." And don't fall into the category of the foolish woman who "tears it down with her own hands" (NASB). What a difference you will make when you stop nagging and complaining, and start assisting your husband in doing what he thinks is best! Think of the difference it will make in the atmosphere of your home if you and your husband work as a team in leading your family in an orderly manner. The world will take notice of this kind of love, harmony, and teamwork, and God will be pleased.

She opens her mouth with wisdom,
and on her tongue is the law of kindness.
PROVERBS 31:26

Envy

Eternal Father, before time You were, and You are,
and You will always be. You have no needs and
are totally sufficient. I need Your help to know that
I am sufficient in Your sufficiency. Yet I admit,
in my sinfulness I often covet what others possess.
Whether it is health, appearance, education, fame,
or fortune, in times of spiritual weakness I envy others.
Help me eliminate envy and constantly be
thanking You for what I do have.
Lord, I know that You have already granted to me
all that is necessary for life. I am blessed with
the greatest possessions of all—an intimate knowledge
of You and Your Son, Jesus, and eternal life.
I praise You that You are my shepherd and
that with Your sufficient daily provision,
I shall want for nothing.

Amen.

From the earliest time of biblical history, envy was a problem for mankind. Cain envied his brother Abel for receiving God's blessing. King Ahab of Israel envied another man's property (1 Kings 21). And the Jewish leaders envied Jesus and His popularity, and later envied the disciples because the crowds were responding to their message about Jesus. In all these cases, the sin of envy or coveting led to murder. No wonder God included covetousness in the Ten Commandments: "You shall not covet" (Exodus 20:17).

The Bible makes it abundantly clear that we are not to set our desires on anything that belongs to someone else. Envying others and their possessions is a pointless exercise for Christians. Why? Because God has already promised to provide everything we truly need. Like the apostle Paul wrote, "My God shall supply all your need according to His riches in glory by Christ Jesus" (Philippians 4:19)—not out of His riches, but "according to His riches." God's riches are limitless, and therefore His provision is limitless. Each day remember to purposefully think about what you do have and be thankful. And stop thinking about what you don't have. Don't fall into the world's trap of envying others. Trust in God's limitless provisions. Pray and strive to be content.

The cure for the sin of envy and jealousy
is to find our contentment in God.
JERRY BRIDGES

Complaining

Dear bountiful Lord God,
it is so easy to allow complaining to become
a habit and a way of life. When my hopes, dreams,
and expectations are not becoming real, I automatically
grumble and complain to anyone who will listen.
God, I confess my complaining as sin because
it shows a lack of trust and gratitude on my part
for Your continuous concern for my well-being.
You have promised You will never abandon me,
and You have provided me with everything I need
to live a godly life. Lord, please forgive me for
my ungrateful heart and renew in me a spirit of
worship and gratitude. May my heart and lips be
a constant fountain of praise and thanksgiving for
Your unfailing grace and provision in my life.

Amen.

In the Old Testament the nation of Israel became free after 400 years of slavery when God delivered them from oppression with signs and wonders. God Himself parted the Red Sea so His people could escape Pharaoh and his mighty army. Yet only three days later, the newly freed captives "complained against Moses" because they had no water (Exodus 15:24). After praising God for the wonders He had performed in releasing them so they could enter a new and promised land (Exodus 15:1-18), their complaints about having no water quickly brushed aside their thanksgiving and praise for all of God's recent miraculous affirmations of His care of His people.

Today we still have very short-term memories when it comes to remembering God's constant goodness. The next time you are tempted to complain about your woes to anyone who will listen, don't. Don't give in to the sin of complaining. Instead, take your concerns to the One and only One who can actually do something about them—to our bountiful Lord God. An even better approach is to choose not to complain and follow the psalmist's example and firmly declare, "I will bless the Lord at all times; His praise shall continually be in my mouth" (Psalm 34:1).

Turn your disappointments into opportunities to praise your faithful, trustworthy—and praiseworthy—God. God did not fail the children of Israel those thousands of years ago, and He will not give up on you today. Let these words from Scripture guide your heart's response to all things:

Rejoice always,
pray without ceasing,
in everything give thanks;
for this is the will of God
in Christ Jesus for you.
1 THESSALONIANS 5:16-18

Frustration

*God, You alone are perfect peace and
the source of peace to all mankind…and to me.
I bless and praise You that Your attitude toward me is
one of peace and not of wrath. When I walk by
Your Spirit, Your peace is like a river that
gently buoys me up and carries me forward.
I come before You today asking for a better day
than yesterday, for a day of handling what comes
my way with Your grace and peace. I will look to
You to calm my chaotic heart and fill it with Your
perfect peace. Help me pull in the reins on all my
breathless activity and stop frantically trying to
function without the peace of Your wisdom and grace.
Show me the way, Lord, and I will walk in it.*

Amen.

Does your day start off like a race against time as you maneuver through a too-long to-do list and unexpected obstacles? Job accurately described this futile and accelerated lifestyle: "My days are swifter than a weaver's shuttle, and are spent without hope" (Job 7:6). No one wants their precious days to pass by swiftly and without hope! If you are rushing in all directions at once, just stop. Breathe. And look upward to God in heaven.

When your priorities are out of whack, you end up madly going through your days with anger, frustration, and failure after failure. There is rarely a sense of accomplishment and hope. Perhaps Gideon experienced frustration when he was asked by God to take on a vastly superior enemy. But once Gideon acknowledged God's power, Gideon lost his fear and frustration and, in response, erected an altar and named it "Jehovah-Shalom," which means "God is peace."

Do you want to experience the peace of Jehovah-Shalom? If so, include one very practical decision in your very busy schedule every day: Put God first. Before your day gets out of hand, curl up in some cozy place and read a portion from your Bible. Fill your mind with God's mind. Begin each day experiencing God's peace. Accept Jesus' offer: "Peace I leave with you, My peace I give to you...Let not your heart be troubled, neither let it be afraid" (John 14:27).

> *You will keep him in perfect peace,*
> *whose mind is stayed on You,*
> *because he trusts in You.*
>
> ISAIAH 26:3

God's Leading

*God, You are not only my reason for living,
my salvation, my comfort, and my provider,
but You are my leader. However, I admit I often
try to make my own path and choose to follow
my own desires or the desires of others. In my heart
I know this is wrong, but all too often I listen to others.
Today I am choosing to follow You, Lord.
I am choosing to delight in Your law and Your ways.
I know this is the harder path, the path few follow,
so when the way gets difficult and I falter,
I will look to You, Father God. Please encourage me.
And please give me the strength and wisdom
I need to follow Your leading.*

Amen.

What would you do if God suddenly called you to a different situation, a different location, a different lifestyle? This happened to Abraham and Sarah in Genesis 12:1. God told Abraham, "Get out of your country, from your family and from your father's house, to a land that I will show you" (Genesis 12:1). Can you imagine? It's definitely easier to follow God's leading when the road is familiar, the difficulties are few, and your destination is known. But what about the times when life isn't all that easy or clear, and God is asking you to follow His leading? Abraham shows us the way: "*By faith Abraham obeyed* when he was called to go out to the place which he would receive as an inheritance. And he went out, *not knowing where he was going*" (Hebrews 11:8)!

Here's a simple test of your willingness to follow God's leadership. On a card or notepad write these words: "Anything, Anywhere, Anytime, At any cost." Could you in all honesty sign the card? God's role is to lead you; your job is to follow Him. So how are you doing? Have you looked into God's wonderful face and whispered, "Truly, dear Lord, where You lead me, I will follow"? Do these words express the deep longing of your heart to team up with God and follow Him anywhere, anytime, at any cost, and do anything He asks?

> *He leads me beside the still waters...*
> *He leads me in the paths of righteousness.*
>
> PSALM 23:2-3

Fear

Father, in the midst of chaos
I come before You with a fearful heart.
Every day news broadcasts and articles feed my fears.
I fear for my safety and for that of my loved ones.
I am fearful of my own mortality as I see so many of
my family and friends facing and succumbing to death.
I am also coming to You with a shameful heart,
recognizing these fears before You as a lack of trust
in Your greatness and power. As I pray now,
I am remembering Your promise that You will
never leave me or forsake me. You have also promised
to stand beside me, watch over me, and ultimately
see me safely home in heaven where I can bask in
the safety of Your presence for all eternity.
Thank You that Your Holy [indwelling] Spirit is
now and always present to settle my heart.
I praise You that even in the midst of frightening
turmoil, I can have peace of heart and mind
because of Your calming presence in my life.

Amen.

Life can be seen as a fearful and challenging experience. It's easy to become fearful of the changing seasons of life, of changing jobs, of changing health, and of a myriad of other life-changing situations. Without God, life can be frightening, but with God, life can be a great faith adventure. This was the situation Joshua was facing as the newly appointed leader of more than two million of God's people. Sensing Joshua's fear, God gave him this reminder: "Have I not commanded you? Be strong and of good courage; do not be afraid, nor be dismayed..." How could Joshua be strong and courageous? With God's command came this assurance: "...for the LORD your God is with you wherever you go" (Joshua 1:9). Just as God was with Joshua, He is with us today, guiding and guarding our every step.

Every day as you face your own special and unique life challenges, you are never facing them alone. Remember this promise of God's presence: "The LORD your God is with you wherever you go." Also remember that if God has called you to a task, His all-sufficient grace will help you accomplish it. "In all these things we are more than conquerors through Him who loved us" (Romans 8:37).

What then shall we say to these things?
If God is for us, who can be against us?

ROMANS 8:31

Godliness

My God, I know that You test
the heart and take pleasure in what is good.
Keep me on Your upright path toward godliness.
Today I willingly offer You
all that I am for this brand-new day.
May my service today be an offering
that is true, pure, and dedicated to You.
O Lord God, may my thoughts and the intent
of my heart reveal my desire for godliness.
Help me always to fix my love and
devotion firmly on You.

Amen.

What does it mean to be godly? Godliness is the respectful awareness of God's sovereignty over every aspect of life. In practical words, it means to "walk in the Spirit, and you shall not fulfill the lust of the flesh" (Galatians 5:16). But before we can walk with God, we must know about God, and that comes from knowing God's revealed truths found in the Bible. Paul wrote of "the knowledge of the truth which is according to godliness" (Titus 1:1 NASB), and Peter declared that God "has given to us all things that pertain to life and godliness, through the knowledge of Him" (2 Peter 1:3).

A godly person is committed to knowing God through reading and obeying His Word. We can read verses in the Bible, but do we obey those verses? The religious leaders of Jesus' day knew the Scriptures. In fact they had memorized vast portions of Scripture. But they did not follow those memorized commands from God. Jesus said, "If anyone loves Me, he will keep My word" (John 14:23)—not just know it or memorize it or read it.

God is asking you to say no to ungodliness and worldly passions and to say yes to living a godly, controlled, upright life. God wants His children to be holy as He is holy. If you are a child of God, godliness should be the ultimate goal of your life. And there is a blessing that comes with this kind of lifestyle, both now and in the future: "Godliness is profitable for all things, having promise for the life that now is and of that which is to come" (1 Timothy 4:8).

God wants the whole person
and He will not rest till He gets us in entirety.
No part of the man will do.

A.W. TOZER

Security

O Lord God, my Protector,
You are my refuge and the fortress for my soul.
You have promised that those who dwell with You
will abide under the shadow of Your almighty presence.
You are my shield in times of trouble.
Because You watch over me, I should not be afraid of
the terror by night, nor of the threats by day.
Though others may fall around me, You assure me
that destruction will not come near me, Your child.
I have put my faith and trust in You, and I know
You will deliver me from evil and show me
the way to safety and rest as promised in Your Word.

Amen.

The kings of Israel were told by God not to amass chariots and horses. Why? Because God knew the kings would be tempted to put their security in these strategic weapons of warfare. King David took God's Word seriously and was obedient to God's warning. David enjoyed great success as a warrior and a leader when he followed the Lord and relied totally on Him for direction and protection. David wrote about his commitment to God in Psalm 20:7: "Some trust in chariots, and some in horses; but we will remember the name of the Lord our God."

Our modern world gives us a false sense of security. We trust in our economy to provide us with plenty of food, clothing, and shelter. We trust in our employer to provide enough money to buy just about anything we need. We trust in our government to keep us safe. We trust in our security systems to keep us from home invasions. Unfortunately, our trust is only as viable as the *objects* of our trust. Any or all of the securities we trust in are fleeting and could fail. King David had the right perspective, which was to remember the name of the Lord our God.

Ultimately, only God can provide true security for you—the security of eternal life through Jesus Christ. Jesus said He would not lose even one person the Father had given to Him (John 6:39). Be careful of falling into the trap of trusting in yourself, your money, your experience, or others—the horses and chariots of this age. Trust in God for true security.

He who dwells in the secret place of the Most High
shall abide under the shadow of the Almighty.
I will say of the LORD, "He is my refuge and my fortress;
my God, in Him I will trust."

PSALM 91:1-2

Steadfast Spirit

*God, You are steadfast forever. Your kingdom is
an everlasting rock that will never be destroyed.
Your rule shall endure throughout all generations.
There is no one better to put my trust in than You.
When my heart and mind are focused on You,
I am at peace, and the cares of this world seem less
threatening and important. But Lord, I confess that
often my heart and mind are not steadfast toward You,
and I do things that are foolish and displeasing
in Your sight. As I seek to be more disciplined,
I will look to You and keep my mind fixed on You.
Grant me the peace You promise
to those who trust in You.*

Amen.

You will be happy to know that you have an attention span
that is less than that of a goldfish! Goldfish have an attention span of nine seconds, while humans lose concentration after
eight seconds. This means we are easily distracted! We may start
a project or make a resolution, but very quickly we are drawn
in another direction. This same lack of concentration applies
to spiritual things. How many times have you resolved to have
a regular prayer and devotional time? How many times have

you tried walking the narrow path of righteousness only to be diverted to the wide path of the sins of the world?

Jesus described this lack of spiritual focus this way: "No one can serve two masters; for either he will hate the one and love the other, or else he will be loyal to the one and despise the other" (Matthew 6:24). James pictured this wavering between worldly things and spiritual things in James 4:4: "Do you not know that friendship with the world is enmity with God? Whoever therefore wants to be a friend of the world makes himself an enemy of God."

What is your focus going to be? Can you accept this challenge from the apostle Paul: "Therefore, my beloved brethren, be steadfast, immovable, always abounding in the work of the Lord, knowing that your labor is not in vain in the Lord" (1 Corinthians 15:58)? If so, God promises to keep you in perfect peace because your heart and mind are steadfast toward Him (Isaiah 26:3).

> *Let us lay aside every weight,*
> *and the sin which so easily ensnares us,*
> *and let us run with endurance*
> *the race that is set before us.*
>
> HEBREWS 12:1

Spiritual Discipline

God, meeting with You
early in the day always makes my day better!
I love our time together, and I want to make
"early time" with You a daily habit and a time to talk
problems and issues over with You in prayer.
I need to receive Your guidance and
instruction through reading Your Word before
the craziness of my day begins. I want to be more
like the psalmist who lifted his heart to You and said,
"My voice You shall hear in the morning, O Lord;
in the morning I will direct it to You,
and I will look up" (Psalm 5:3). This discipline of
putting You first, Lord, will give me focus for my day.
Thank You for the fresh energy and clarity of mind,
for the strength and wisdom only You can give me
each morning as I lay my day before You.

Amen.

If you are always running behind, why not cultivate the discipline of getting up early? Do you remember Joshua's master plan to defeat Jericho? God's precise instructions to Joshua to tear down the wall of Jericho included getting up early every day and marching around the besieged city (Joshua 6:12-15).

And this strategy resulted in a resounding success! An even better example of the discipline of getting up early comes from the life of Jesus: "Now in the morning, having risen a long while before daylight, He went out and departed to a solitary place; and there He prayed" (Mark 1:35).

Try this exercise: Calculate what time you need to get up in order to have some devotional time with your heavenly Father. Then set your alarm—and, of course, get up when you hear it! As you turn out the light each night, center your thoughts on what you desire to accomplish for the Lord tomorrow. The time you spend praying and planning in the early part of the day will lead you to a master plan that works. So up and at 'em! Approach your day with fresh energy, with delight, and with anticipation. This is a spiritual discipline that will not only bless you, but also many others as you approach the day with a plan—God's plan.

God, You are my God; early will I seek You;
my soul thirsts for You; my flesh longs for You
in a dry and thirsty land where there is no water.

PSALM 63:1

Generosity

Gracious Father,
You have blessed me exceedingly abundantly,
beyond all that I could ever ask or think!
I praise You, Father, and thank You profusely.
All that I have comes from You. Help me be
a wise steward of what You have entrusted to me, and
open my eyes and heart to the needs of those around me.
May I use what You have blessed me with to bless others.
I want to be a faithful steward—
careful with my money and generous to
those who could use some help.

Amen.

Before Jim and I and our two girls became a Christian family, our focus had been on worldly pursuits...and our checking account was maxed out. Yet, having received the greatest gift of all—Jesus Christ, we knew we needed to follow Jesus' instructions when He said, "Freely you have received, freely give" (Matthew 10:8). We started the process of turning our focus away from the world and toward the things of God. But as time went on, I knew I needed to do more.

I vividly recall the day I wrote in my prayer journal, "Pray to be more generous." You see, I was a bookkeeper, accounting for every penny we had or spent. But after assessing my spiritual life, I discovered I could use a l-o-t of improvement in this area of giving. So every day I began asking God for opportunities to give. I prayed for open eyes and an open heart that would recognize the needs of others.

The amazing results from nurturing a generous heart are that people hear the Good News of Jesus Christ, people in need are helped, and some people accept Christ as their Savior and enjoy eternal life! I cannot do all these things, but I can give and fund and pray for organizations and people who can.

And here's another added benefit to your generous spirit. You will have the joy of knowing you were obedient to Christ's command to "freely give." And you will know many in need have been helped. So, be generous with your money. God will bless you. As the saying goes, "You cannot outgive God." Paul put it this way:

My God shall supply all your need
according to His riches in glory by Christ Jesus.
PHILIPPIANS 4:19

Fear of Others

Lord, You are the creator and sustainer of all things.
There is no force on earth or in all the universe
that You do not control. By Your Word the worlds
were formed, and by Your Word they are sustained.
Nothing will happen in my life that You do not know
about and permit. So, dear shepherd of my soul,
help me trust in You and resist fearing what others
may say about me, think about me, or do to me.
Thank You that through Your sustaining grace,
nothing and no one, "neither death nor life,
nor angels nor principalities nor powers,
nor things present nor things to come,
nor height nor depth, nor any other created thing,
shall be able to separate us from the love of God
which is in Christ Jesus our Lord"
(Romans 8:38-39).

Amen!

Many women are intimidated by the negative reactions of others about their Christian beliefs and their personal standards. Do you have people in your life who say negative things about you, cut you off, leave you out, or ridicule your beliefs? This is when we can begin to hesitate or even fear being around them. The Israelites surely understood these feelings. Ten spies reported that the people of the Promised Land were giants, living in walled cities and impossible to defeat (Numbers 13:27-33). But two other spies, Joshua and Caleb, reassured the people not to fear the threat and power of the pagan inhabitants of the Promised Land. They said, "The LORD is with us. Do not fear them" (14:9).

Detractors are a fact of life, but we are not to hate them or fear them or fight them. No, we are to cry out to God. Luke 6:28 says, "Bless those who curse you, and pray for those who spitefully use you." The truth is, your foes will never achieve victory. God is watching over you, and He promises to avenge you if needed (Deuteronomy 32:35). No one can frustrate God's plans or His promised protection and victory for your life. Don't fear as the Israelites did, who allowed their fear of the enemy to rob them of God's blessings. Follow Joshua and Caleb's admonition and be strong. Boldly believe "The LORD is on my side; I will not fear. What can man do to me?" (Psalm 118:6).

The fear of man brings a snare,
but whoever trusts in the LORD shall be safe.
PROVERBS 29:25

Wisdom

Father, You are "the Alpha and the Omega, the Beginning and the End." Your Word is the source of all the wisdom I will ever need for any and every situation, and all I have to do is ask You for it! But Lord, all too often I fail to seek Your wisdom. In my pride I think I know the answers and fail to find out what Your Word says. It is my prayer that I will quickly look to You and Your Word for guidance for whatever choices, decisions, and responsibilities I will face today. I want to possess Your wisdom and receive Your instruction. I need Your wisdom, and I am asking for it now.

Amen.

Wisdom is often thought of as knowledge. Maybe this will help clear up any confusion: Knowledge is information, whereas wisdom is knowledge applied. You can be a "smart" person but also be unable to make good decisions. A wise woman takes the knowledge she possesses and makes the right choices.

Hearing about the "wise woman" might give the impression such a woman must be very old. Yet wisdom does not have anything to do with age. Any woman of any age can pray any day and throughout all her days for wisdom. It is possible to have a life characterized by peace and joy, by order and meaning—all marks of a life of wisdom. How can this kind of life be yours? Proverbs 9:10 gives the essence of what is required: "The fear of the LORD is the beginning of wisdom, and the knowledge of the Holy One is understanding."

God possesses both knowledge and wisdom, and you are living according to God's wisdom whenever you do what His Word says. If you have a heart for God and read and apply His Word, you will be growing spiritually and making wise decisions. You will "keep your heart with all diligence" and "ponder the path of your feet" and "remove your foot from evil" (see Proverbs 4:23-27). You will be living a life of wisdom one minute at a time, one thought at a time, one decision at a time.

If any of you lacks wisdom, let him ask of God,
who gives to all liberally and without reproach,
and it will be given to him.

JAMES 1:5

Worldliness

God, You are wholly set apart from
the world that You have made, and yet You are
actively concerned for my spiritual condition as
I live in the world You have made. I am amazed by
the many ways You encourage my spiritual growth and
give my life value. And yet at times I selfishly
slip into thinking that the world is not so bad.
Dear Lord, I know I am called to be in the world
but not of the world. Help me hold lightly the things
of this world and hold tightly to Your ways of living.
Give me strength to resist my flesh and the vanities
that surround me. Please work in my life today.

Amen.

Meet Eve, the first person to experience worldliness. God had provided Adam and Eve with everything they could possibly want. Well, *almost* everything. God had withheld one thing—the fruit of the Tree of Life. Notice how Eve succumbed to worldliness: "So when the woman saw that the tree was good for food, that it was pleasant to the eyes, and a tree desirable to make one wise, she took of its fruit and ate" (Genesis 3:6).

Worldliness is being concerned with worldly affairs while neglecting spiritual things. Eve was willing to neglect spiritual things like communing with God and obeying Him because of the lure of the one forbidden fruit. The apostle John summed up worldliness in this way: "All that is in the world—the lust of the flesh, the lust of the eyes, and the pride of life—is not of the Father but is of the world" (1 John 2:16). John's description looks very much like Eve's path toward sin, doesn't it?

The Bible has a great deal to say about worldliness, and none of it is good. "Do not love the world or the things in the world. If anyone loves the world, the love of the Father is not in him" (1 John 2:15). "Adulterers and adulteresses! Do you not know that friendship with the world is enmity with God? Whoever therefore wants to be a friend of the world makes himself an enemy of God" (James 4:4). Fortunately, the remedy for this problem is found in Colossians 3:1-3:

> *If then you were raised with Christ,*
> *seek those things which are above,*
> *where Christ is, sitting at the right hand of God.*
> *Set your mind on things above,*
> *not on things on the earth.*

Gossip

*Lord of love and truth, I acknowledge that
my heart is deceitful and desperately wicked,
and I have been guilty of gossip more times than
I care to admit. Please help me nurture a heart of love
for others and the wisdom to know when to speak
and when to stay silent. As I step into this day,
I am purposing to pray before I speak, and to choose
to encourage with my words instead of gossiping.
My heart's desire is to honor You by being a woman
who loves and uplifts and blesses others, a woman
whose words are acceptable in Your sight, O Lord.*

Amen.

Godliness and maliciousness simply do not go together. But women often get caught up in behavior that does not honor God. For instance, gossip. We hear something about someone and pass it on because it's news, or funny, or shocking. We like being the source of information, the woman-in-the-know. But gossip can easily and quickly transform into slander. In the Bible, the term "slanderer" is used in reference to people such as Judas Iscariot, the man who betrayed Jesus. "Slander" is also a title used for Satan. This is company a woman after God's own heart wants nothing to do with.

Two women show us the evils of ungodly and unchecked gossip. Potiphar's wife slandered the righteous man Joseph because he refused her sexual advances, and Joseph was locked in a prison for three years (Genesis 39–40). And Queen Jezebel set into motion false accusations that the righteous Naboth had blasphemed God, which led to Naboth being stoned to death! Why did she do this? So her husband, King Ahab, could possess Naboth's land.

These are extreme examples of the consequences that result when we choose to open our mouths in sinful lies and malicious gossip. As James notes: "Out of the same mouth proceed blessing and cursing." Then he exclaims, "These things ought not to be so" (James 3:10).

An obvious cure for gossip is to develop a heart of love—love for the Lord, love for His Word, love for His people, love for the truth. Then you won't gossip, because you would never knowingly slander someone you love. Instead you will speak only "what is good for necessary edification, that it may impart grace to the hearers" (Ephesians 4:29).

Whoever guards his mouth and tongue
keeps his soul from troubles.
PROVERBS 21:23

Godly Change

*Heavenly Father, Your ways are perfect, true,
and upright. You are holy, and You have instructed me
to be holy as You are holy. Thank You that this holy and
righteous transformation began in me with
the acceptance of Your Son, the Lord Jesus Christ,
as my Savior. I know that godly change is
an ongoing process that will not be completed
until I see You face-to-face. I want to purposefully
submit myself to this process day by day so I am
further conformed to the image of Jesus.
Help me yield to the transforming power
of Your Holy Spirit today and
begin again tomorrow.*

Amen.

If you are like many women, you don't do well with change. You like your routine! You like it when everything stays just as it's always been. You delight in flowing through your days without much thought, operating on autopilot. Having a routine that seldom changes is good for your daily schedule, but it can be a deterrent to your spiritual life. If you are a believer, change should be a part of your life. When the Holy Spirit took up residence in your life at salvation, He began His process of "sanctification" in you—the process of becoming more like your Savior, Jesus Christ. The apostle Paul described this process: "The Lord—who is the Spirit—makes us more and more like him as we are changed into his glorious image" (2 Corinthians 3:18 NLT).

Unfortunately, you—and all believers—sabotage this spiritual transformation process when you allow sin to dominate your life and "grieve the Holy Spirit" (Ephesians 4:25-32). When you fail to confess your sin, a different kind of change occurs: Rather than being "transformed" into the likeness of God, you become "conformed to this world" (Romans 12:2).

Do as the Bible says and be quick to confess your sin. Keeping a clean slate with God frees the Holy Spirit to do His work in you, changing and transforming you into the image of your glorious Savior. The process is not easy, and you will always have to contend with your flesh. But by God's grace, you and those around you can witness and glory in the change that is taking place in your life...starting today!

Therefore, if anyone is in Christ, he is a new creation;
old things have passed away; behold, all
things have become new.

2 CORINTHIANS 5:17

Fulfilling Your Potential

*Lord God, You have saved me and
planted seeds of hope and potential in me.
For this I praise and thank You! Your Word says
that by faith I can accomplish great things for You.
That, precious Lord, is the deepest desire of my heart and
the aim of my life. When I am discouraged or fearful,
I need only to remember that the power of the
Holy Spirit lives in me and that He is ready to
use me to do His will and benefit others.
Please give me the strength and confidence
I need to step out in faith and trust that,
because of Your power and grace, I can be used
by You and do what You ask of me.*

Amen.

Created by God, the human mind and body can accomplish amazing things. Today we continue to be amazed by advancing technology and human potential and intelligence. Have you thought about your own potential lately? Do you ever think that you have nothing to offer? Please don't buy into this lie. Don't give up on the truth of God's plans for you. After all, *you* are "fearfully and wonderfully made." *You* are one of God's "marvelous" works (Psalm 139:14)!

You may think you are ordinary...which is exactly the kind of person God is looking for! An ordinary person is one who can be used by God to do extraordinary things for Him. Explore the story of Gideon in Judges 6. The Lord sent him to help save Israel. But Gideon said, "How can I save Israel?...I am the least in my father's house." And God's reply? "Surely I will be with you!" God saw something special in Gideon, something Gideon wasn't even aware of—potential! God took a fearful coward and transformed him into what is described in the Bible as a "mighty man of valor."

When God calls you to do or become something beyond your ability, you can rely totally on His strength and power. Today and each and every day of your life remember, recite, and believe the truth of Philippians 4:13: "I can do all things through Christ who strengthens me." What seemingly impossible task is God asking of you so you can move toward living out your full potential?

[God] is able to do exceedingly abundantly
above all that we ask or think,
according to the power that works in us.
EPHESIANS 3:20

Growing

*Dear God in heaven who does great, unsearchable,
and marvelous things without number, thank You that
as I read Your Word, I can gain a better understanding
of who You are—the great and wonderful Creator of
the universe. When I read my Bible, open my eyes
so I can grasp Your wisdom and principles,
and incorporate them into my life. Please continue
to remind me that true spiritual growth comes
as Your truths are established and
rooted in my heart.*

Amen.

It's easy to think you don't have time to read the Bible. Your
schedule is packed before you even get out of bed. And it's
easy to think, "If I don't read my Bible, I will have more time
for other things." Then we wonder throughout the day why
things go so badly! Could it be because we followed our schedule and failed to follow Jesus' advice to "seek first the kingdom
of God and His righteousness"? We also miss out on the added
blessing that comes from living by this priority—"and all these
things shall be added to you" (Matthew 6:33)!

Job understood the importance of communing with God
when he said, "I have treasured the words of His mouth more

than my necessary food" (Job 23:12). Job was saying that he would rather miss eating than miss spending time with his God. Your time spent in the Bible plays a significant role in your spiritual growth. Peter put it this way: "Desire the pure milk of the word, that you may grow" (1 Peter 2:2).

God wants you to grow in your knowledge of Him, and that growth comes as you read your Bible. So begin today to develop the habit of reading God's Word every day. Begin by setting your alarm to get up just a few minutes earlier than your usual time. It's been calculated that if you spend just ten minutes a day, you can read through your Bible in one year. That doesn't sound like much time, but it's definitely enough to make sure you are growing. As you read the quote below ask yourself, *Wouldn't "the life of ever upward growth" be a good goal for me?*

> *More difficult still, apparently,*
> *is the life of ever upward growth.*
> *Most men attempt it for a time, but growth is slow;*
> *and despair overtakes them.*
>
> HENRY DRUMMOND

God's Will

*Dear heavenly Father, You are ever present and
You watch over all things. Nothing happens that
You do not already know. You know the beginning
from the end. You know what is best for me.
From before the foundation of the world,
You knew Your will for me. But often I forget to ask
what You desire for my day and my life.
Please give me courage and patience as
I look into Your Word and search for understanding
as to Your good and perfect will for my life.
I trust You to guide me to make right choices—
Your choices—so I live out Your will.
This is the prayer of my heart:
"Not my will, but Yours, be done."*

Amen.

Wouldn't it be ideal to have God's direction revealed to you as He did for many Old Testament saints? God appeared in a dream, or spoke personally, or sent a prophet to speak His will to His people. Well, you can be thankful that God is still faithful to show us His will. In Deuteronomy 10:12-13, it is impossible to miss what God says is His will: "What does the LORD your God require of you, but to fear the LORD your God, to walk in all His ways and to love Him, to serve the Lord your God with all your heart and with all your soul, and to keep the commandments of the Lord and His statutes which I command you today for your good?"

This passage of Scripture is one of many that will help you understand more of God's will for your days and your life. Reading His Word regularly and humbly seeking direction through earnest prayer are important keys to understanding God's will. God's Word sets the boundaries of His will. And prayer then helps you bring your will into line with God's will. Repeat this process as you face each new day packed with events and responsibilities. Keep depending upon God and looking to Him for guidance and direction. As you follow God, He will help you stay on the path of His will.

> *The will of God is not something you add to your life.*
> *It's a course you choose.*
> *You either line yourself up with the Son of God...*
> *or you capitulate to the principles which*
> *govern the rest of the world.*
> ELISABETH ELLIOT

Marriage

Lord, You performed the very first marriage
when You brought Adam and Eve together,
showing mankind that marriage is sacred to You and
should be to me. Keep me pure and totally devoted to
my husband. Help me to always think of him as
my best friend, my closest companion and confidant—
my beloved. I ask for Your help in changing and
fine-tuning my priorities so I can be more available to
help, encourage, comfort, and pamper my husband.
Bless our marriage, Lord God. Bind our hearts
together in love for one another—Your kind of love.

Amen.

Perhaps you've heard it said that marriage is the union of two selfish people who want their own way. Maybe that's why marriage is always a work in progress. Marriages are dynamic: They are always changing as families grow with children, as jobs change, and as physical changes arrive with the seasons of life.

To keep these changes working for you, make sure God is your greatest priority. Your love for God and your understanding of His love for you is vital to your marriage because, as Jesus prompted, "This is My commandment, that you love one another as I have loved you" (John 15:12). Next is your spouse. After God, your husband is to be your greatest concern. He is to receive the largest investment of your love, time, and energy. In Judges 13 we witness the beautiful relationship Manoah and his wife had. They enjoyed the blessing of being best friends, and together they experienced extraordinary moments: grieving infertility, meeting and talking with an angel of the Lord, raising a strong-willed son, and mourning his death.

Titus 2:4 says to love your husband. This means that you love him as your best friend, a cherished brother, an intimate life mate. If this is not what you are experiencing in your marriage, check your priorities. Ask God to work first in your heart and to help you *want* to be your husband's closest companion and best friend. Then rearrange your life so there is more time for him, and for the two of you to work on rekindling your friendship. You'll be glad you did.

Marriage is a total commitment
and a total sharing of the total person
with another person until death.
WAYNE MACK

Praying—God's Way

*Lord Jesus, You have said in Your Word that
if I ask anything in Your name, You will hear and
answer my prayer. Dear Savior, search my heart and
its motives when I pray. Help me always to ask whether
the things I request are Your will or something I selfishly
want to see accomplished. Draw me near to You
so I can listen for Your direction and pray with
godly purpose. Today I pray specifically that
my thoughts, heart, motives, and prayers will
be pure and pleasing in Your sight.
Thank You, Lord. I'm listening!*

Amen.

Knowing how dependent the disciples had become on Him, Jesus spent the evening before going to the cross reassuring His disciples that He would provide them with the necessary resources to accomplish their work on earth without His presence. He was going to send a "Helper"—the Holy Spirit—who would be a personal presence in each of their lives. In addition, He promised that "whatever you ask in My name, that I will do" (John 14:13). Praying in Jesus' name meant that the disciples should make sure their prayers were consistent with what Jesus would want, not what they might selfishly desire. The answers to their prayers would come based on Jesus' merit, not on any merit of the disciples.

Jesus was telling us there is a right way to pray—God's way. For instance, we love to pray for the health and well-being of ourselves or others. And we love to pray for protection and provision. There's nothing wrong with these requests, but what is behind these prayers? Often we are asking for what we think is best for us and our loved ones, rather than what would best pursue God's glory.

As you pray, be sure to lift your motives before the Lord. When you bring your requests to Him, ask Him to take a close look at your heart. Be willing to acknowledge any selfish or sinful motives and adjust them to what you know is His will. Your goal is to match your motives with what God, in His Word, tells you is pleasing to Him.

Prayer, or talking one-on-one with the God of the universe, is an incredible privilege. So purpose to pray daily. Pursue a life of prayer. And participate in the blessings of seeing God's will done both in and around you.

Our Father in heaven, hallowed be Your name.
Your kingdom come, Your will be done
on earth as it is in heaven.
MATTHEW 6:9-10

Friendships

Precious Lord, I thank You that
You are a friend of sinners, including me.
As You were a friend to Your disciples, You are also
a faithful friend who stays close to me—closer than
a brother or sister. I want to exhibit and extend that
same kind of loyal and faithful friendship to others.
I want to be a friend who encourages and
exhorts my friends to love You and trust You more.
God, please give me the strength and conviction
to be a better friend to those around me,
a friend who is faithful, loyal, and wise.

Amen.

In the book of 1 Samuel we see a lasting and faithful friendship between young David and Jonathan, the son of King Saul. When King Saul sought to kill David, the friendship between these two young men continued to be strong. Even at the most difficult times, they each promised their forever friendship and support to the other.

In the New Testament, we learn more about friendship from the relationship between two women—Mary, who was a teenager, and her much older relative Elizabeth (Luke 1). Because they were both on the same godly path, they encouraged and assisted each other. They were friends who helped each other move forward through a difficult but exciting time.

It's hard to find a true friend in the way David and Jonathan, or Elizabeth and Mary, were to each other. A true friend is described in Proverbs 18:24 as one who sticks closer than a brother or sister. This proverb also says, "A man who has friends must himself be friendly."

The starting point to having friends—the right kind of friends—is first to be a godly woman yourself—a woman who loves the Lord and can give wise counsel and prayer support. Can others trust you with their hopes and their troubles? Are you available, open, and willing to listen? Do you keep your word? Can you love others in the same way Jesus loves you? Can you follow the advice of Proverbs 17:17: "A friend loves at all times"? What can you do today to cultivate and nurture your godly character so you are the kind of woman who will be a wise and faithful friend?

He who walks with wise men will be wise,
but the companion of fools will be destroyed.
PROVERBS 13:20

Forgiveness

O Lord, You are good and ready to forgive and abundant in lovingkindness. In Your goodness and mercy and by the death of Your Son, Jesus, for sin, You have removed my sins from me as far as the east is from the west. I praise Your holy name that they are banished and remembered no more. Receiving and experiencing Your gracious forgiveness of my sins makes me want to be sure I forgive others. Grant me Your grace to forgive, forgive, and forgive again.

Amen.

How is it possible for a holy, righteous God to forgive sin? As one of the Old Testament prophets testified of God, "You are of purer eyes than to behold evil, and cannot look on wickedness" (Habakkuk 1:13). This means that for us to have a relationship with a holy God, Jesus' death on the cross had to take place (2 Corinthians 5:18), and we must accept Christ's death as payment for our sins.

The apostle Paul's past was filled with hatred for Christians, resulting in brutality and great harm done toward Christians in the early church. He even labeled himself the "chief" of sinners (1 Timothy 1:15). And yet Paul included himself in this amazing statement of forgiveness: "In Him [Christ] we have redemption through His blood, the forgiveness of sins, according to the riches of His grace" (Ephesians 1:7). Paul understood that God's forgiveness is limitless and based on His limitless grace.

With this limitless grace, sometimes it's tempting to take advantage of God's forgiveness and assume He will overlook your sin. However, because of your relationship with God, you will want to confess all sin as quickly as possible. Remember, as you continue to confess, He continues to forgive (1 John 1:9).

It is truly amazing that God's forgiveness is complete. It's permanent and limitless. Unfortunately, some people, and maybe even you, believe that some of their sins are too big or too bad for God to forgive. If this describes you, remember that God's grace is bigger and greater than all your sin. There may be consequences from your past sins, but God's cleansing love and forgiveness can see you through them. Accept God's forgiveness. Embrace His mercy. Count on His unfailing love. Trust in His powerful promise that His forgiveness is forever.

Blessed are those whose lawless deeds are forgiven,
and whose sins are covered.

ROMANS 4:7

Commitment

*It is a challenge to keep my focus and
attention on You, Lord. The desires of the flesh
constantly pull me toward the world.
Lord, help me shun the things of this world.
Help me focus my attention on the things above
where Christ, my Savior, dwells. Revive my heart and
renew my love for You, Your Word, and Your people.
With Your help I want to focus fully on Christ,
to commit my body, soul, and spirit to Him
and to be transformed into His image.*

Amen.

When your relationship with Jesus began, you were asked for a commitment. Jesus said to those who follow Him both then and now, "If anyone desires to come after Me, let him deny himself, and take up his cross, and follow Me" (Matthew 16:24). But it's easy to get distracted with other things—some good, but some questionable. A man in the Old Testament was facing this same spiritual crossroad of commitment. His name was Joshua, and he had to decide whether to continue in his commitment to follow after the gods and pleasures of the world around him or to follow God. His choice? "As for me and my house, we will serve the LORD" (Joshua 24:15).

It is oh so subtle, but too often we fail in our commitment to forsake all and follow Jesus. It is not always intentional. We simply begin to lose our passion and commitment. Slowly and little by little, the world begins to pull us away from our first love, the Lord Jesus. Examine yourself and your commitment to God. If this is where you are today, or if this is the direction your spiritual life is moving, quickly follow Joshua's example and choose to follow and "serve the Lord." Ask God to restore your love, to heat up your passion for Him and His Word. Be willing to live for Christ and show the world your commitment to joyfully and passionately serve the one, true, living God and His Son, the Lord Jesus Christ.

The Christian life is not adding Jesus to one's own way of life but renouncing that personal way of life for His, and being willing to pay whatever cost that may require.
JOHN MACARTHUR

Compassion

*I thank and praise You, Lord, that Your love and
compassion toward me are new every morning.
Regardless of my sinful attitudes and my disobedience,
You are a faithful God whose compassion toward me
never ceases. Because of Your love and concern,
I know You will help me when I call out to You.
Ignite in me that same love and compassion
You have for those around me who are physically
sick and weak, who could use a cup of cold water
in Your name. But especially give me a heart of
compassion for those lost in sin. I want to use every
opportunity to pray for those without Christ and
show them Your lovingkindness and compassion.*

Amen.

Parts of the prayer above come from Lamentations 3:22-
23: "Through the LORD's mercies we are not consumed,
because His compassions fail not. They are new every morning; great is Your faithfulness." These encouraging words were
poured out of the prophet Jeremiah's heart in the midst of the
sin and sorrow that surrounded the destruction of Jerusalem. As
Jeremiah viewed the devastation, he experienced hope, knowing

that God's compassion would see him and a remnant of His people past the ruin.

Throughout the Bible we see God responding when His people call out to Him. Maybe there is some sin in your life that you think God will not forgive. God's steadfast love and compassion are greater than any sin. You only need to call out to God in repentant sorrow, and the mercy of God will surround you and give you relief from your burdens.

Follow your Lord's example as seen in the Gospels. Jesus showed compassion for a demon-possessed man who lived among the tombs (Luke 8:27), for a diseased woman (Mark 5:25), for the family of a dead child (Matthew 9:18,24-25), and for a widow who had lost her only son (Luke 7:13). When you recognize someone's needs, do you act? Many people have physical and spiritual needs you can meet, either by yourself or with the help of others. Having experienced God's compassion yourself and seen it modeled for you by Jesus, every day is an opportunity for you to pass God's compassion on to others.

I would rather feel compassion
than know the meaning of it.
THOMAS AQUINAS

Faithfulness

You are faithful, O Lord, and greatly to be praised.
Regardless of my actions, You are faithful to keep
Your promise to never leave me or forsake me in
this present life. You also assure me that I will
enjoy Your eternal presence in the life to come.
Until that time, I want to respond in obedience to You.
Help me to be faithful to Your Word,
to be consistent in my walk with You and steadfast
in my trust in Your love and grace toward me.

Amen.

God is faithful" (1 Corinthians 1:9) is a description of God's character. We should never doubt that God has and will fulfill all His promises, both to the righteous and the unrighteous as King Solomon stated in 1 Kings 8:56, "There has not failed one word of all His good promise." As God's child you should desire to possess this rock-solid quality of faithfulness. And God makes your faithfulness possible when you are obedient to walk in His Spirit.

Faithfulness means you are loyal, trustworthy, and reliable, first and foremost in your relationship with God. It means you are faithful to His Word and His will for your life. And it means you are loyal and trustworthy toward others. This quality and fruit of faithfulness becomes vital when you see that God calls you as a woman to be "faithful in all things" (1 Timothy 3:11). In other words, you show up—even early so others won't worry. You follow through on whatever you have to do. You keep your word—your *yes* means *yes,* and your *no* means *no.* You keep your commitments and appointments. You can be counted on to be where you said you would be, doing what you said you would do.

From God's Word it is obvious that faithfulness is a major distinction of Christian women and a quality God uses to benefit the church and the body of Christ. So take a quick inventory of your Christian walk. Let God's definition of faithfulness stretch your understanding of the fruit of faithfulness (Galatians 5:22), a fruit that is so needed in our world today! Ask God for His strength as you cultivate His faithfulness in your life.

Women must likewise be dignified,
not malicious gossips, but temperate,
faithful in all things.
1 TIMOTHY 3:11 NASB

Courage

Great Shepherd of Your sheep,
I will fear no evil,
for Your rod and staff protect me.
Just as You gave victory to the children of Israel
when Moses held up his rod as Your banner,
so today You give me victory through my banner,
the Lord Jesus Christ. I never need fear life or death or
any person because Your banner of protection is over me.
Help me rely on Your strength and
be strong in You and the power of Your might.
May I be quick to put on the armor of God,
so I will be able to stand firm against the evil one.
This is my prayer today, O Lord.

Amen.

Moses had a rough beginning as the leader of God's people. His leadership was questioned, and the people complained and became fearful of dying of starvation and of thirst. But miraculously, each time they lacked food or water, God provided! Then they discovered a greater enemy—"Amalek came and fought with Israel" (Exodus 17:8). With Amalek having already defeated Israel once (Numbers 14), God gave Moses directions: He was to hold up the rod that had parted the Red Sea, and the Israelites would defeat their enemy. After the victory was won, Moses built an altar and called its name "The-Lord-Is-My-Banner" (Exodus 17:15).

As Moses's rod was the symbol of God's banner of salvation in the Old Testament, Jesus' death on the cross has become our banner of salvation (John 12:32). And with that salvation, we can have courage and confidence. Jesus gave this assurance to His disciples when He said: "In the world you have tribulation, but take courage; I have overcome the world" (John 16:33 NASB). Jesus' promise strengthened His disciples—and you and all believers. With these words Jesus assured us that He had victory over the world, and we don't need to be afraid of the future. The world is a scary place, and persecution is a daily occurrence for Christians around the world. Your faith is being challenged daily on every side. But do not fear. Jesus secured your victory on the cross.

Be strong and of good courage;
do not be afraid, nor be dismayed,
for the Lord your God is with you wherever you go.
JOSHUA 1:9

Creativity

Dear God, creator and maker of the heavens and the earth and all that is within Your creation, I thank You for the creative spark You have placed in mankind. As You gave men the Spirit-filled abilities to be artistic craftsmen to build the tabernacle for worship, so You have given men and women down through the centuries the ability to create beauty. I thank You that You have blessed me with both spiritual gifts and physical skills. Help me discover, develop, and use my creative abilities to honor You, serve You, and bless others.

Amen.

When it comes to gifts and abilities, our tendency is often to think that somehow in God's creative process, He made an exception or overlooked us. Or when gifts and abilities were given out, the "greater" ones were given to people in leadership. If you have these kinds of thoughts, you are mistaken. Our creative God has given His creativity to all mankind. But for Christians these gifts and abilities are to be focused on God's purposes. For example, God gave two men, Bezalel and Aholiab, the abilities needed to accomplish His will for building the tabernacle (Exodus 31:2-6).

The book of Proverbs has much to say about women and their skills, gifts, and abilities. For instance, in chapter 31 of Proverbs, God describes a woman who possessed great wisdom and outstanding skills and abilities. She is described as an excellent gardener, a weaver, a seamstress, an upholsterer, a merchant, a manufacturer, an importer, a manager, and a landowner. And don't miss the fact that she was also an exemplary wife and mother. But at the core of her amazing achievements was her reverence for God (Proverbs 31:30).

Like the giftedness and abilities that resided in this great lady, you too are created by the Creator in His image. Like the woman of Proverbs 31, develop a deep reverence for God and His Word. Ask Him for greater discipline so you can discover, develop, and use your God-given talents. Ask Him to help you embrace the industry, integrity, diligence, resourcefulness, and creativity that made her a remarkable woman. The world is waiting for your creative contribution!

Give her of the fruit of her hands, and
let her own works praise her in the gates.
PROVERBS 31:31

Dealing with Loss

*God of all comfort, today I praise You that
You give strength to the brokenhearted and aid to
those who are in need. You bring sweet relief to
those who are in pain. You protect and defend
the weak and provide for those who suffer.
Often I feel alone and sad with the loss of
something or someone that is familiar and precious
in my life. Yet I know You are always present
and will fill the emptiness I am experiencing
with Your love, grace, and peace.
Thank You that my losses give me opportunities to trust
You and experience a greater measure of Your grace.
When I am weak, You give me Your strength to carry on
and to also comfort others who are experiencing loss.
Thank You for Your love and concern.*

Amen.

If you are not experiencing loss at this time, this blessing is truly worthy of giving praise to God! But for many, loss is a present reality—loss of a family member, loss of health, loss of a job, loss of a home through financial setbacks, fire, or disaster. If this is where life finds you today, you have a choice to make: You can allow yourself to be consumed by your loss, your pain, and your sorrow, or you can choose to be consumed by God and His mercy, His comfort, and His grace. Let these words comfort you in your situation: "Even to your old age, I am He, and even to gray hairs I will carry you! I have made, and I will bear; even I will carry, and will deliver you" (Isaiah 46:4).

In his day, Paul addressed the topic of widows in the church and the loss of husbands, the greatest of all personal relationships. He said, "Now she who is really a widow, and left alone, trusts in God and continues in supplications and prayers night and day" (1 Timothy 5:5). Whatever the loss, either past or present, you too must trust God in the same way those widows were instructed to do. Call upon God's strength to help you bear your burden of loss. Then ask God to turn your loss into an opportunity to minister His grace to others who are suffering loss.

Blessed be the God and Father of our Lord Jesus Christ,
the Father of mercies and God of all comfort,
who comforts us in all our tribulation,
that we may be able to comfort those who are in any trouble,
with the comfort with which we ourselves
are comforted by God.
2 CORINTHIANS 1:3-4

Devotion to God

Father, You are omniscient!
You see, know, and understand all that is in my heart.
Nothing in me or in my life is hidden from You.
I welcome Your all-seeing eyes. It makes no sense to
try to hide any thoughts or actions from You.
In fact, Father, it amazes me that even though You
know everything about me, including the worst,
You still love me. This moves me to want to give
You my total and wholehearted devotion.
Help me be a living sacrifice, fully dedicated
to serving You and Your people.
Blessed be Your holy name!

Amen.

Devotion to God and to our Lord Jesus Christ is something God's people desire. And we can make great progress in living up to these desires when all is going well. But how do we respond during the tough times, the trying times, the terrible times?

To encourage your devotion to God when things are not going well, consider the women who were present at the cross of Jesus: "Mary Magdalene and Mary the mother of Joses observed where He was laid" (Mark 15:47). On this gruesome day, these and other women endured witnessing their friend and Savior's ghastly crucifixion. They stayed at the cross when the disciples had fled. They followed Jesus' body to the tomb, returning after the Sabbath with spices for preparing His body for burial.

These women could not speak in Jesus' defense before the Jewish leaders of the Sanhedrin. And they could not appeal to Pilate or the Roman governor, or stand against the crowds, or overcome the power of the Roman guards. But they did what they could do—they could see to Jesus' needs to the very end. Because of their devotion, they were blessed to be the first people to witness the resurrection of their beloved Jesus.

Your devotion to the little things is just as important as to the big things. God is not asking a big thing from you, like dying for Him, though that might be His will for you in the future. What He is asking is that you be devoted to Him in the little things, such as being "a living sacrifice, holy, acceptable to God" (Romans 12:1). Like these exemplary women at the cross, tend to the little things. Take advantage of every opportunity you have to do what you can for Christ and His people and His purposes.

He who is faithful in what
is least is faithful also in much.
LUKE 16:10

Doubt

Eternal Father, You are the same yesterday and today, and will be the same tomorrow. Not one word of all Your promises has ever failed—or will fail— to come to pass. The grass may wither and the flower may fade, but You are from everlasting to everlasting, and Your Word will abide forever. Your unfailing nature reminds me that I don't need to worry or doubt Your sovereign knowledge and control over every area or issue I will ever face throughout the days of my life. When I falter and begin to doubt You and Your many promises to care for me, please strengthen my faith, Father. I do believe. Help my unbelief.

Amen.

In the Bible the concept of doubt was introduced in the early days of creation. In Genesis 3 we learn that the serpent, Satan, tempted Eve to sin by persuading her to doubt God's Word and His goodness. He said to the woman, "Has God indeed said, 'You shall not eat of every tree of the garden'?" (Genesis 3:1). By questioning God's character, Satan tempted Eve to disregard all that God had given her and to focus instead on the one thing she could not have. Eve's doubt was not sin, but her doubt led to the sin of disobeying God's command not to eat of that particular fruit.

Doubt is the result of a lack of trust. What is the solution? We resist doubting by practicing trust. It may be a little more difficult to practice trust in human relationships, but trust should never be an issue when it comes to God. God has proven Himself trustworthy. Whether it is biblical history or His personal relationship with you through Jesus Christ, you can trust God. You already know this, but maybe you can identify with the wavering faith of a father when he asked Jesus to heal his son. The distraught father "cried out and said with tears, 'Lord, I believe; help my unbelief!'" (Mark 9:24).

Thank God that when your faith is strong, disappointment and doubt disappear. As you trust in your heavenly Father and His unfailing promises, your heart will no longer be troubled, and your doubt will become a thing of the past.

Faith is not belief without proof,
but trust without reservations.
ELTON TRUEBLOOD

Discernment

God, You know everything!
You discern the hearts and intents of all men.
You expose the darkest of secrets with the searchlight of
Your truth. Nothing escapes Your penetrating insight.
Your judgments are true and righteous. You have
said that if I receive Your Word, and treasure
Your commands within my heart, and cry out for
understanding, You will give me Your wisdom—
the ability to discern good from evil. I praise You
that when I am obedient to You, Your wisdom
enters my heart, and discretion preserves me and
helps me make right choices—Your choices.

Amen.

Everyone has made bad decisions and wrong choices. And we have all said or done foolish things—things we wish we could go back and do over. Unfortunately most, if not all, of those decisions and choices cannot be taken back, and we must live with their consequences.

But what if we could reduce the number of bad decisions by using the wisdom and knowledge of God? Proverbs 2 tells us how:

First, you must value the source of that wisdom and discernment—God's "words" and His "commands" (verse 1).

Next, you must read and apply what you are reading. "Incline your ear to wisdom, and apply your heart to understanding" (verse 2).

Also, you cannot be casual about wanting discernment. It must be a passion. You must "cry out for discernment, and lift up your voice for understanding" (verse 3).

Finally, seeking and searching for God's direction must be a lifelong pursuit. "If you seek her as silver, and search for her as for hidden treasures; then you will understand the fear of the Lord, and find the knowledge of God" (verses 4-5).

What is the product of all your efforts? "Discretion will preserve you; understanding will keep you, to deliver you from the way of evil" (verses 11-12). Wisdom and discernment are available to you at any time. All you have to do is look to God's Word. Seek and search for wisdom with all your heart for all your days. Read the chapter in Proverbs that corresponds with that date. The God of all wisdom will fill you with His wisdom.

How blessed is the man who finds wisdom and the man who gains understanding....
She is more precious than jewels;
and nothing you desire compares with her.

PROVERBS 3:13,15 NASB

Temptation

*Faithful Shepherd, You have asked me to
be in this world, and You have promised to
guard me from the evil one. I am surrounded by
the temptations of worldly pursuits. God, grant me Your
"won't power" today. I need it just about every minute.
It is easy to justify my behavior, but I know it is
hurting me, crippling my walk with You, and
shortchanging the people in my life who depend on me
to be a woman of integrity and excellence.
Needless to say, Father, I need Your strength.*

Amen.

Wars and the rumors of war are a reality of the day and age we live in. And, as you know all too well, there is also a war going on inside you. The apostle Paul described this internal battle with these words: "I find this law at work: Although I want to do good, evil is right there with me. For in my inner being I delight in God's law; but I see another law at work in me, waging war against the law of my mind and making me a prisoner of the law of sin at work within me" (Romans 7:21-23 NIV).

But, praise God, we have the assistance of the Holy Spirit living in us, helping defend us against both our flesh and Satan's evil attacks. As we live in the Spirit and seek His resources and self-control, we can withstand temptation and not succumb to the deeds of the flesh. This is victory over temptation!

When temptation comes your way, quickly call on God for His strength, and then, whatever you are tempted to do—don't do it! Don't give in to emotions, to cravings, to urges, to the opinions of others. Don't think or do what you know is against God's Word. Don't rationalize sinful behaviors and harmful words and actions. When the Bible speaks of self-control, it means the ability to say no. It is willpower that expresses itself in "won't power."

No temptation has overtaken you
except such as is common to man;
but God is faithful, who will not allow you
to be tempted beyond what you are able,
but with the temptation will also make the way of escape,
that you may be able to bear it.

1 CORINTHIANS 10:13

Kindness

Your lovingkindness is precious to me, O God.
"Because Your lovingkindness is better than life,
my lips shall praise You" (Psalm 63:3)! I thank You
that Your kindness continually ministers to me.
Without it I would have trouble living in this world.
I want the love and compassion You have shown me
to be reflected in my relationships with others.
Purify my heart so I can walk by Your Spirit and
bless others with Your kindness, a fruit of Your Spirit.

Amen.

In the midst of the constant cruelty displayed by the nations that surrounded Israel, we see a bright ray of kindness extended by a merciful woman to the prophet Elisha (2 Kings 4:8-10). This lady lived in Shunem, a town Elisha passed through on his preaching tours. Noticing that Elisha had nowhere to stay, this "notable" woman persuaded her husband to provide a place for the prophet whenever he passed through the region. She saw a need and responded in kindness.

Being kind sounds simple and easy, doesn't it? But it's not always easy, especially when we run into people who are rude, selfish, or simply mean. Jesus said that when we do good to these kinds of people, we show ourselves to "be sons of the Most High.

For He is kind to the unthankful and evil" (Luke 6:35). The Bible also calls us to "put on a heart of...kindness" (Colossians 3:12 NASB). God issues another call to kindness in 2 Timothy 2:24. Here the apostle Paul tells us how to act toward those who are not Christians: "The Lord's bond-servant must not be quarrelsome, but be kind to all" (NASB). Galatians 5:22-23 teaches us that when we walk in the Spirit, we manifest the fruit of the Spirit, which includes kindness.

How do you see yourself? Are you kind just to those who are kind to you? Do you have a heart of compassion and kindness toward others? As you prepare yourself spiritually for each day, pray for opportunities to show kindness, especially to your family. Then, just as you would put on a coat or jacket to leave your house, put on an attitude of kindness and demonstrate that you are a child of the Most High God.

The person who sows seeds of kindness
enjoys a perpetual feast.
AUTHOR UNKNOWN

Consistency

*You, O Lord, never change. You are consistent
in all Your ways, never deviating from Your purposes
and plans. I bow before You today, desiring to
be more like You—faithful and consistent, especially
with prayer and time in Your Word. More times than I
want to admit, I become overwhelmed by commitments,
obligations, and responsibilities, and fail to follow
through on my most important priority—
spending time with You. I am purposing to
be more consistent, starting today.
My prayer is to be consistent and not quit,
give up, or dismiss the tasks You call me to.
Thank You in advance for Your help.
I need it!*

Amen.

One of God's attributes or character qualities is faithfulness. He never deviates from His purposes or plans. The psalmist says of God, "He remains faithful forever" (Psalm 146:6 NIV). And God the Son is described as "the same yesterday, today, and forever" (Hebrews 13:8). As Christian women God's faithfulness must be a part of our character. This means being consistent in our daily life, which exhibits God's presence in us. When we are walking in the Spirit, we display faithfulness, a fruit of the Spirit (Galatians 5:22-23).

Being consistent and faithful to follow through with your tasks and responsibilities is difficult and a real challenge. Maybe that's why being consistent is such a rare quality, and why it's easy to quickly give one—or all—of these excuses and rationalizations:

- ~ I had a rough night, and I'm too tired to do it.

- ~ I'm too busy today. This can wait. I'll do it tomorrow.

- ~ This task is too great, and I'm already overwhelmed. Let someone else do it.

- ~ It's not that important, so who cares if I don't do it?

- ~ Hey, I don't want to do it, so I won't do it!

Meet Phoebe. Talk about being consistent and faithful! Phoebe is described in Romans 16:1 as "a servant of the church." She had proven herself to be a faithful servant in the church body. As a result of her dependability, Paul chose Phoebe to hand-deliver an important document to the Christians in Rome. Ask God to help you cultivate a life of consistency. Then, like Phoebe, people can count on you to accomplish what needs to be done.

And P.S.: The letter Phoebe carried was the book of Romans!

Be steadfast, immovable,
always abounding in the work of the Lord.
1 CORINTHIANS 15:58

Health

You, God, are the God who heals.
You are the great physician. You demonstrated this
when Your Son walked this earth and healed
every kind of sickness and disease.
When I have a loved one or know of someone
who is facing health issues, I pray to You
because I know that You have the power to heal.
I also know that illness is a part of life,
and even though You are able in Your power and
grace to heal, I recognize that You may have
a greater purpose in mind for those who are suffering.
Thank You that I can entrust my health and
that of my loved ones into Your divine care.
In Your wisdom and love, do what You know is best.

Amen.

When the children of Israel left Egypt, they failed to trust God when there was no water. He had already told them that if they would obey His commands, He would take care of them and keep them free of disease. He stated, "I am the LORD who heals you" (Exodus 15:26). With these promises from God Himself, there should have been no worries.

At times we are like the Israelites. When things are going well, we praise God. When life isn't going our way, as with health issues, we become bitter and angry and find ourselves murmuring against God. We question, "Why are You doing this to me, God?" Our health or lack of it becomes a test of our trust in God's goodness and mercy. Rather than asking, "Why, Lord?" we should be asking, "How can I glorify You through this illness, Lord?" or "What are You wanting to teach me through this trial, Lord?"

Even more important than your physical health is your spiritual health. Set a goal to develop the apostle Paul's bold faith when he declared, "I take pleasure in infirmities...For when I am weak, then I am strong" (2 Corinthians 12:10). Trusting God during times of difficulty will make you spiritually strong, which is more important than your physical health. Through Christ's death, you have spiritual health insurance—eternal health insurance! Through Christ you are healed of the eternally fatal disease of sin.

He Himself bore our sins in His body on the cross,
so that we might die to sin and live to righteousness;
for by His wounds you were healed.

1 PETER 2:24 NASB

Devotion

*God Almighty, Your might and power are evident as
I look in all directions. Your creation of both
the heavens and the earth is beyond comprehension.
Your bounty and riches and the fullness of Your grace
are overwhelmingly evident in my daily life!
How could I ever turn from looking fully to You
for life and direction and help?
Dear Lord, convict my heart of sins
that continue to linger in my life. I want to do as
You have commanded in Your Word. I want to turn
from my selfish ways and keep Your commandments.
I want to follow Your righteous path, to please You.
I want to be able to declare,
"My soul follows close behind You"
(Psalm 63:8).*

Amen.

Second Kings 17 tells the story of a people who had drifted toward sin and away from God. The children of Israel had forgotten the promises of God and His holy Word. When the admonition of God came to them, it was loud and clear: "Turn from your evil ways, and keep My commandments and My statutes" (verse 13). But like their ancestors, the people ignored

God's counsel. They failed to learn from history, and tragically repeated it. And we are guilty of doing the same thing! Instead of repenting and learning from our bad behavior and choices, and devoting ourselves to follow God more closely, we tend to repeat the same mistakes over and over again.

How many times have you been guilty of ignoring God's counsel and turning away from God and toward sin? There is a simple solution to this problem, and that is to surrender your heart, mind, and will to God each day by making a fresh daily decision to renew your devotion to the Lord. How is this done? By spending time praying to Him, praising Him, and worshipping Him. By reading His Word and dedicating yourself to follow hard after Him. By memorizing and hiding His Word in your heart.

Take an inventory of what you usually think about, dwell on, and entertain in your mind. As Proverbs 23:7 says, "As [a man] thinks in his heart, so is he." Whatever is in your thoughts and heart will show up in your behavior. Devotion to God begins in your heart. Make this psalm from David your own: "Let the words of my mouth and the meditation of my heart be acceptable in Your sight, O Lord, my strength and my Redeemer" (19:14).

Present your bodies a living sacrifice,
holy, acceptable to God,
which is your reasonable service.
ROMANS 12:1

Questioning God

Oh, the depths of the riches both of Your wisdom and knowledge, almighty and all-knowing God! Your ways are unsearchable, and Your judgments and decrees are past finding out. Your ways are not my ways, and often I don't understand what is happening in my life. Forgive me for questioning Your judgments concerning me. I know that my times are in Your hands. Unfortunately, I occasionally forget this truth. I praise You that my every day and every struggle were known by You before I was born and that You are always with me, even during the darkest times.

Amen, and thank You!

Job was described as "the greatest of all the people of the East" (Job 1:3). He had everything. Yet in a very short period of time he lost everything—his sons and daughters, many servants, vast lands, herds of livestock—including his health! As Job sat scraping painful sores and boils off his skin, his wife gave him this discouraging advice: "Do you still hold fast to your integrity? Curse God and die!" (Job 2:9).

You may not suffer the same kind of hardships Job faced, but you will experience a lot of tough times in life. When you do, don't fall into the trap of thinking God has made a mistake or that He turned His back and walked away when you needed Him. In the midst of despair, rein in your thoughts and refuse to blame or blaspheme God.

The Bible describes God as being perfect in wisdom—and that includes His timing. What is happening in your life right now? If these are tough days, remember to acknowledge that God has planned your life...even if it doesn't seem like it right now. Psalm 18:30 says, "As for God, His way is perfect; the word of the LORD is proven; He is a shield to all who trust in Him." These truths will help you fight the good fight of faith and keep you from anger, bitterness, and resentment. And they will give you hope.

When life becomes difficult, don't doubt God or believe the negative things people say about Him. Instead, trust Him—completely, fully, and without doubt. Remember that God is the author of every moment of your life, and you are in His perfectly capable hands.

> *As for God, His way is perfect;*
> *the word of the LORD is proven;*
> *He is a shield to all who trust in Him.*
>
> 2 SAMUEL 22:31

Making Good Decisions

Great God and my shepherd,
as You guided Israel like a flock,
guide me as one of Your sheep toward
making right and righteous decisions.
I am trying, Lord, to follow Your leading,
but I have a long way to go. And Lord,
I do want to follow Your leading.
I am excited to pursue actions and plans that
are pleasing to You and move me further toward
being the kind of person I long to be—
a woman after Your own heart.
I know that as I am faithful to
read Your Word and pray, You will give me
clear and perfect direction that will put me on
Your path to discovering Your wisdom.

Amen.

Not a minute goes by that you aren't forced to make decisions. As you listen to someone speak (and the operative word is "listen"), you must carefully decide how to answer. And when there's a crisis and you have to make a quick decision, you must be as careful as possible.

When there are unexpected quiet moments in the whirlwind

of life, put that time to good use and prepare for the next challenge. Sit and enjoy reading your Bible. Pay special attention to the lives of the people in the Bible who faced important decisions, crises, and conflicts. One example is King Josiah, who reigned from the age of eight and introduced reforms to a people lost in sin (2 Kings 23). One of the first wise decisions Josiah made was to make "a covenant before the LORD, to follow the LORD and to keep His commandments and His testimonies and His statutes" (verse 3). Maybe that's why the Bible makes this declaration about King Josiah: "Now before him there was no king like him, who turned to the LORD with all his heart, with all his soul, and with all his might" (verse 25).

Make your first wise decision each day to spend time in your Bible so you may follow the Lord and keep His commandments. Put God in first place. Arm yourself with His wisdom and instruction. As you gain a better understanding of God's Word, and His wisdom becomes your wisdom, making good decisions will become easier, and there will be less potential for making really big mistakes.

Trust in the LORD with all your heart,
and lean not on your own understanding;
in all your ways acknowledge Him,
and He shall direct your paths.

PROVERBS 3:5-6

Spiritual Maturity

Almighty God, when You first appeared to Abraham,
You instructed him to follow You and walk with You.
If Abraham did so, You promised, "I will bless you and
make your name great; and you shall be a blessing"
(Genesis 12:2). Today I come before You and ask for
Your blessing. I realize I am still a work in progress.
Each day I desire to grow spiritually, O Lord.
I want to be more disciplined. As I make a greater
effort to follow You and walk with You as Abraham did,
please work in my life, and work on me.
Please continue Your refining and
perfecting process in my life.

Amen.

Please be patient—God is not finished with me yet." This is a popular positive saying that reflects the truth that you are a work in progress and will one day be perfect. In Philippians 1:6 we find this encouraging promise: "Being confident of this very thing, that He who has begun a good work in you will complete it until the day of Jesus Christ."

In Jeremiah 1:5, God called Jeremiah to serve Him as a prophet. In verse 6, however, Jeremiah tried to give God several reasons why he could not be a prophet—"Ah, Lord GOD!

Behold, I cannot speak, for I am a youth." But God had already told Jeremiah, "Before I formed you in the womb I knew you; before you were born I sanctified you; I ordained you a prophet to the nations."

Jeremiah did not need to worry. God was not finished with him. If fact, God was just beginning to mold Jeremiah into the man who would serve Him as a mighty prophet.

The powerful truth that each believer in Christ is a work in progress is seen in Romans 5:8. Here the apostle Paul reminds us that "God demonstrates His own love toward us, in that while we were still sinners, Christ died for us." Christ did His part and began the process of your spiritual maturity, which will be complete when you arrive in heaven. In the meantime, do your part. Grow spiritually by reading your Bible, by praying, and by being obedient to the Spirit's leading.

As you therefore have received
Christ Jesus the Lord, so walk in Him,
rooted and built up in Him and established in the faith
as you have been taught,
abounding in it with thanksgiving.
COLOSSIANS 2:6-7

Joyfulness

I am instructed in Your Word, Lord, to approach You as God, my exceeding joy. I know that when I get bogged down and my days seem dreary and mundane, I must remember to turn to You as my true source of joy— not the emotion of joy but to the fruit of a life which submits to Your Spirit's control. Thank You that the moment I take my mind off my problems and look to You, my sorrows and distress are transformed into joy. Open my mind and heart to Your amazing gift of joy, Your beautiful fruit of the Spirit!
Thank You, precious Father.

Amen.

Life has its ups and downs, and sometimes it seems like it's more down than up. It's easy to want to just give up. What is the solution? It is the Word of the Lord. God's Word can cheer you like nothing else can. As the prophet Jeremiah reported, "Your word was to me the joy and rejoicing of my heart" (Jeremiah 15:16). If you read the book of Jeremiah, you will realize that Jeremiah was not talking about the emotion of joy, which responds to circumstances. Jeremiah was hated, abused, persecuted, and had his life threatened. No, Jeremiah's joy was based on his understanding of God as recorded in His Word. He knew where true joy came from, and so did the psalmist who praised: "I will go to the altar of God, to God my exceeding joy; and on the harp I will praise You, O God, my God" (Psalm 43:4). God is the source of true joy, and He wants to give you His joy. Only in Him will "your sorrow...be turned to joy" (John 16:20).

So rush to the Word of God. Take all your sorrow, troubles, and discouragement with you. God's peace and perspective are available to you right in His Word, even when grief and gloom are part of your day. The Bible will teach, correct, instruct, and guide you. And, yes, it will cheer you up, bring you joy, and give you hope. A woman after God's own heart has a passion for His Word. Spend your time learning about your God and Savior. *He* is where you will find true joy that will sustain you for your life's journey!

Rejoice always, pray without ceasing,
in everything give thanks;
for this is the will of God in Christ Jesus for you.
1 THESSALONIANS 5:16-18

Trials

Mighty God, You have said in Your Word that in this world I will have troubles, and it has happened. Lord, I have carried the weight of several of these troubles for too long. You also said that I can come to You with my burdens and You will give me rest for my troubled soul. Thank You for Your strength, Your concern, and Your love in wanting to share my burdens—for wanting to take them away…and for being able to! Today I kneel before You and place my burdens into Your strong and capable hands. I praise You that You can do what I cannot do.

Thank You, thank You, and amen!

Trouble is a fact of life. You may be facing a difficult time in your life right now. But don't lose heart. God knows all about you and the issues you are facing. It is a fact of faith that you can ease your troubles with prayer. In the book of Jeremiah, you can read about the many difficulties this faithful prophet faced. But despite his suffering, Jeremiah's faith and confidence in God were revealed in his prayers when he pronounced, "The Lord is with me as a mighty, awesome One" (Jeremiah 20:11).

When trials come your way—and they will!—ask God to do

what you cannot do. Refuse to cave in to despair. Instead, do as James advises and view your trials in a positive way: "Count it all joy when you fall into various trials, knowing that the testing of your faith produces patience" (James 1:2-3). God allows trials to give you greater strength. James adds these words of instruction for times when you are facing troubles: "Is anyone among you suffering? Let him pray" (James 5:13).

Praising God for His goodness and lovingkindness, and praying for strength during your trials and troubles gives you confidence in the Lord, the "mighty, awesome One," and in His ability to take care of you. Let the "mighty, awesome One" fight your battles. And rejoice that He will judge and make things right. Don't lose heart—just bring your heart to God.

If we desire our faith to be strengthened,
we should not shrink from opportunities
where our faith may be tried,
and therefore, through trial, be strengthened.

GEORGE MUELLER

Forgiving Others

Gracious Lord, You are good and abundant in lovingkindness, ready and willing to forgive all who call upon Your name. I thank You that through Your Son, Jesus, I have unlimited forgiveness. Your Word tells me that the same forgiveness You have extended to me should be shared and extended to others. Help me follow Your divine example and forgive those who have hurt me. Soften my heart into a forgiving heart so I can reap the blessings of thanksgiving, pure joy, and freedom that come when I forgive as I have been forgiven.

Amen.

One of the greatest blessings of God's forgiveness is being able to pass on that same mercy to others. Forgiving others who hurt us, whether physically or mentally, is not a natural human response. But an unforgiving heart is a hard, bitter, angry and ugly heart. This is what happens when we harbor wrath and malice against those who have caused us pain. The writer of Hebrews warns us to deal with an unforgiving heart, "lest any root of bitterness springing up cause trouble, and by this many become defiled" (Hebrews 12:15). The key to freedom from anger and bitterness is prayer and forgiveness. Only then will a heart be freed from anger and be free to love.

The obvious next question is, how many times should I forgive another person? That is the question Peter asked Jesus: "Lord, how often shall my brother sin against me, and I forgive him? Up to seven times?" Jesus said to him, "I do not say to you, up to seven times, but up to seventy times seven" (Matthew 18:21-22). In other words, Jesus was saying that forgiveness should be limitless.

Your willingness to forgive others is an indication that you are a true believer—one who has been forgiven by God. It's been said that forgiveness from God is man's deepest need, and forgiving others is man's highest achievement. Such forgiveness should begin in your own home, toward those who are closest to you. But don't stop there! Who else needs your forgiveness? You probably don't even need to think about it. Quickly go and forgive—as you have been forgiven.

If Jesus forgave those who nailed Him to the cross,
and if God forgives you and me,
how can you withhold your forgiveness from someone else?
ANNE GRAHAM LOTZ

Work

Did you know that work was not the result of man's fall into sin? No, work began with creation. God did His creative work for six days and then rested on the seventh day. Work was also conducted in the Garden of Eden. For instance, Adam's work included giving "names to all cattle, to the birds of the air, and to every beast of the field" (Genesis 2:20). And Eve's work was to be "a helper suitable for" her husband (Genesis 2:18 NASB). Work is part of man's nature and is necessary for fulfillment and continued existence.

In 1 Chronicles 26:1-19 you will find a narration about the temple gatekeepers that gives you an inspiring lesson on doing your work heartily. At first glance it may seem like the work of the gatekeeper was nothing special. But in ancient times it was a task reserved for the Levites, those men set aside by God to tend to the temple of God. It was a huge responsibility and a great honor.

What is your attitude toward work? Consider these instructions from Colossians 3:23: "Whatever you do, do it heartily, as to the Lord and not to men." "Heartily" means giving your work everything you've got as to the Lord, not for anyone else who may be watching. Serve the people in your life with your all-out best efforts, but let your motivation always be to please the Lord and not to receive accolades or attention. Are you a wife or mom? Serve and tend to your husband and children heartily. Are you in college? Throw yourself into it and give your all. Do you have a job? Serve your employer heartily, "for you serve the Lord Christ" (Colossians 3:24). Work with an attitude that is positive, productive, and points others to the God you represent.

Therefore...whatever you do,
do all to the glory of God.
1 CORINTHIANS 10:31

Complacency

Father God, Your Word tells me to be content.
You also tell me to keep on keeping on, to move forward
so that I move toward a more active, vibrant,
growing faith and greater ministry to Your people.
Help me distinguish between contentment and
complacency. I don't want to stand still when I am
meant to be growing in my knowledge of You and
in my service for Your causes. Thank You for showing me
the way and energizing me to follow. Because You are
by my side, I can face forward and reach beyond
my comfort zone for the prize of Your upward call.

Amen.

Are you content right where you are? If so, is that a good thing? Paul said he had "learned...to be content" when he wrote about his personal needs and desires (Philippians 4:11). But in Philippians 3:13-14 the apostle Paul admonished us as followers of Christ not to be content with our spiritual condition. Paul urged us to "press toward the goal for the prize of the upward call of God in Christ Jesus." The apostle Peter wrote that we are to constantly be growing "in the grace and knowledge of our Lord and Savior Jesus Christ" (2 Peter 3:18). Being comfortable may feel good, but God is urging us to move toward a different goal. Too much comfort invites us to watch the race rather than participate in it. Paul calls us to be active, to get into the race and reach "forward to those things which are ahead" (Philippians 3:13).

And just in case even thinking about a new challenge fills you with fear, fear not! Paul wrote these words of encouragement for those times when you are fearful: "I can do all things through Christ who strengthens me" (Philippians 4:13).

In the Scriptures you will find the strength and wisdom you need to achieve new goals in your spiritual and personal growth. So what are you waiting for? Don't be complacent. Don't be lazy. Don't be afraid. And don't be satisfied with your present spiritual state. Take to heart David's advice to his son Solomon before Solomon began to build God's temple:

Be strong and of good courage, and do it;
do not fear nor be dismayed,
for the LORD God—my God—will be with you.
He will not leave you nor forsake you,
until you have finished all the work.

1 CHRONICLES 28:20

Peace

Father in heaven, Gideon addressed You as "Lord of peace," and so do I. He built an altar to worship You. Father, today I worship You. Knowing You are the Lord of peace comforts me. It helps me to replace my needless stress with the peace and stillness I can find as I seek You in Your Word. Revive me as I rest beside Your peaceful, still waters. Lord of peace, renew and energize me to take care of my responsibilities with a gentle and quiet spirit—with a heart of peace.

Amen.

Do you ever wonder, "Where can I go to find peace?" Our world is a frantic place to live in, and unfortunately, many times we are our own worst enemy. Does this list sound familiar?

- Busyness is number one on our daily list of challenges. There is never enough time—and always "just one more thing" to do.

- Responsibility is next, weighing us down and causing us to worry.

- Tension is on the list too. We wonder what the next crisis will be...because there will be one!

~ And don't forget stress, the mother of anxiety, fear, headaches, insomnia, ulcers, and other physical ailments.

But here's some very good news! Psalm 23:2 says God "leads me beside the still waters." Still waters! Can't you just sense yourself relaxing as you imagine resting beside cool, clear, still waters?

The God of peace knows your need for peace, and He provides it. He ensures the restoration and the calm you need to continue fulfilling His will. God does His part. But there is something you must do: Seek Him with all your heart, soul, mind, and strength. This is precisely the focus of 2 Chronicles, chapter 14. Although this chapter recounts battles and military achievements, the emphasis is in verse 7: The people of Judah received rest and peace because Asa, their king, sought the Lord and declared, "He has given us rest on every side." Each day hand over the anxiety that problems, stress, and responsibilities bring into your life. Give them to God in prayer and seek refuge in Him. Rest in His promise of peace:

Peace I leave with you, My peace I give to you;
not as the world gives do I give to you.
Let not your heart be troubled, neither let it be afraid.

JOHN 14:27

Patience

Father of all grace, my heart hurts today as
I struggle to wait patiently for You to reveal Your will
in some weighty matters in my life. I don't understand
some of the "whys" in my situation, but I do know that
I must wait patiently on You to unveil Your good and
acceptable will for me. While I am waiting,
please grant me the grace to endure—to continue to do
what must be done, to take care of my home and family,
to be faithful in my work, to tend to the dailies.
Most of all, help me to remain faithful to You in
my spiritual walk—to be a woman of prayer,
to not lose hope, to praise you no matter what—
to continue to have faith in You, love You, trust You,
and follow You with all my heart.

Amen.

As a child you were probably told many times, "Honey, you have to learn to wait." Learning to wait is a part of growing up and of growing in spiritual maturity. If we want to be women after God's own heart, we must let God set the pace...even if that involves waiting.

Imagine having to wait a year or two—or even longer—for something that you want right now. Do you find it difficult? And what if you had to wait 25 years? This is what happened with Sarah. Initially, God told Abraham that He would make him a great nation—meaning he would have children (Genesis 12:1-3). Yet it was 25 years later that a son was finally born to Sarah (Genesis 21:2). That's a lot of waiting! Unfortunately, while waiting, Sarah became impatient and tried to "help God out" by giving her servant Hagar to Abraham to father a child. Sarah's impatience caused great strife in her family and great strife that continues among the nations to this day.

As a believer in Christ, you can wait because you have access to God's fruit of the Spirit, patience. When you have to wait, wait patiently. God has a plan that will unfold in His timing. Don't try to "help God out" by taking matters into your own hands. And while you are waiting, do something positive that brings you closer to God, such as talking to God in prayer and enjoying His written Word. In the end you will be glad you did.

I waited patiently for the LORD;
he turned to me and heard my cry.

PSALM 40:1 NIV

Reputation

God, You have called me to be an ambassador who represents You to a watching world. It is sobering to realize there are people who are watching my behavior, and I may be the only Bible they will ever read! I hope and pray that my life is giving a somewhat accurate picture of Your love, mercy, and gracious redemption. May I live a more dedicated life today and every day so my actions honor and glorify Your holy name. Help me as I seek to faithfully serve You and represent You with integrity.

Amen.

The famous King David of the Old Testament no doubt had an amazing impact on Israel and its surrounding countries. His life is a testimony to the blessings that come from being obedient to God. However, even with all his accomplishments, one singular act of sin—David's affair with Bathsheba, which led to another sin, his plot to kill Bathsheba's husband—tarnished his life, his family, and his nation for generations to come. Here are some principles to keep in mind so you don't lose sight of the importance of a good reputation:

Principle 1: Understand that sin cannot be hidden forever. First Timothy 5:25 tells us that all sin will be revealed, whether it is "clearly evident" now or is made known at the final judgment. Examine your heart. Are there any areas of sin you need to confess and give up?

Principle 2: Understand that good deeds will not be hidden forever. Although they are not always recognized immediately, good deeds done with godly motives and unto the Lord will ultimately come to light (1 Timothy 5:25).

It's been said that a good reputation takes a lifetime to develop but can be lost in a moment. This is why it is so vital that you live defensively. Always be on guard for any behavior that would mar your purity and reputation. Pray regularly to remain faithful to God's instructions in His Word and to exhibit godly behavior.

As a believer in Christ, you are Christ's representative. The people you encounter will make judgments about Christ based on your actions. Purpose and pray to be a true and worthy example of Christ's love and character, a walking advertisement!

If I take care of my character,
my reputation will take care of me.
DWIGHT L. MOODY

Thankfulness

Today, Lord, I worship You with the psalmist's words: "O LORD, our Lord, how excellent is Your name in all the earth" (Psalm 8:1); "I will praise You with my whole heart" (Psalm 138:1). Today, Lord, I will tell of all Your marvelous works. You alone are worthy to be praised. I don't say it enough, but I am eternally thankful to You for my salvation, my family, and for each new day. I praise You for Your peace that comforts my worried heart. Help me continue to grow in my walk with You and to pray, praise, share, sing, and live with an attitude of gratitude.

Amen.

In the Bible we are instructed more than 300 times to praise God and be thankful. How can we express our thanks? Think on all you have been given in Christ—your salvation, the presence of the Holy Spirit in your life, and God's provision for you as His child. And don't forget to thank Him for the marvelous gift of His Word—the Bible.

Then ensure that God's Word is a part of every area of your life—your heart, your thoughts, your speech, your goals, and your desires. Rejoice with psalms, hymns, and spiritual songs, and let your gratitude sound forth. David expressed thanks after successfully delivering the ark of God to the tabernacle in Jerusalem. In his "Song of Thanksgiving" he praised the name and works of God: "Oh, give thanks to the Lord! Call upon His name; make known His deeds among the peoples! Sing to Him, sing psalms to Him; talk of all His wondrous works!" (see 1 Chronicles 16:8-36).

The more you develop a heart of gratitude and dwell on God's goodness, the more you will praise, sing, talk, and be thankful for Him. When your life includes thankfulness for your relationship with God and the blessings you enjoy in Him, you will want to reach out to as many people as you can. You will want to minister to as many people as you can, in as many ways as you can. You will want to "declare His glory among the nations, His wonders among all peoples" (1 Chronicles 16:24). Be thankful. Let the whole world know God is worthy of praise.

Giving thanks always for all things to God the Father,
in the name of our Lord Jesus Christ.
EPHESIANS 5:20

Worship

*Dear Father, You are worthy of all honor and glory.
Before You and only You every knee will ultimately bow.
Because I have life through Your Son, I can worship You
now and throughout my day, anytime, and anywhere.
And I can worship with Your people! Help me to
understand more fully the importance of the
fellowship and worship in my church. I want to be
as reverent and attentive in my worship as
Your saints were who worshipped at Solomon's temple.*

Amen.

In 2 Chronicles chapters 2–7 God places great emphasis on the temple built by Solomon. This focus began with King David, Solomon's father, who gathered the materials and gave Solomon instructions for building the temple (see 1 Chronicles 28-29). Why all the emphasis? Why all the care? Why all the many details? Because this temple was to become the center of worship for God's people and a place of prayer. The sacrifices that would be offered there would remind the people of the seriousness of sin. It was also to be a symbol of God's presence and His forgiveness and mercy.

Today, God has given you and His people a new place to focus your worship and prayers and to be reminded of the importance of worship and the seriousness of sin. That place is the local church—not a physical building but an assembly of worshippers. During this present church age, believers in Christ are "*living* stones, [who] are being built up [as] a *spiritual* house, a holy priesthood, to offer up *spiritual* sacrifices acceptable to God through Jesus Christ" (1 Peter 2:5).

You can rejoice today that you are a part of the living stones and a part of the body of Christ and that you have the privilege of faithfully and regularly coming together for worship. So—rejoice!

Let us consider one another...
not forsaking the assembling of ourselves together,
as is the manner of some,
but exhorting one another, and so much the more
as you see the Day [of Christ's return] approaching.
HEBREWS 10:24-25

Fulfillment

Lord Jesus, You are the author and finisher of my faith.
You have led the way into heaven as the forerunner
for me and all those who have believed in You
for salvation. From eternity past You have had
a sovereign plan for my life. Lord, help me see myself
as You do—as one of Your children who is on
her way to fulfilling Your grand plan. I am a person
You created with a specific plan and purpose...
before the foundation of the world!
I pray to live out Your plan, and I thank You
for the hope and the future
You have in mind for me.

Amen.

Are you wondering if life has passed you by? Does everyone's life seem to have significance but yours? Well, that may be how the Jews felt after they were sent away into captivity. As they looked at their surroundings in Babylon, the place of their captivity, life looked bleak. But God was not through with His people. He had a plan for them and encouraged them with this promise: "I know the thoughts that I think toward you...thoughts of peace and not of evil, to give you a future and a hope. Then you will call upon Me and go and pray to

Me, and I will listen to you. And you will seek Me and find Me, when you search for Me with all your heart. I will be found by you" (Jeremiah 29:11-14).

Always remember you are a child of God! Ephesians 2:10 describes you as "His workmanship." Be encouraged that God has a grand plan and purpose for your life even though at times things look bleak. Focus on God's promises of peace, of the future and hope He has for you. Don't give up, because God has not given up on you—and He never will.

To discover more about the plans God has for you, take time to look at Scripture, and the more, the better! God's plans are not a secret, so set a daily appointment and read your Bible with great anticipation. Expect to learn more about His will on every page of the Bible. You will be overjoyed when you discover and step into the future and the hope God has for you, His precious child.

Now hope does not disappoint,
because the love of God has been poured out in our hearts
by the Holy Spirit who was given to us.

ROMANS 5:5

Time Management

*Father of time and eternity, You have placed me
on this earth for a specific amount of time.
My days, months, and years are a priceless gift
from You and an invaluable resource. Thank You for
Your gift of time. I know I complain too much
about not having enough hours in my day, and yet
at the same time I know You never give me more than
I can handle. You always give me the time I need to
handle what You want me to do. My heart's desire is
to be more focused, more efficient, and more
consistent in managing my time. Teach me to be
a better steward of the minutes, hours, and days
You have graciously granted to me.*

Amen.

Today, before you launch out into an ocean of frantic activity, take a few minutes to analyze your time, a resource given to you by God. You cannot stop time, and once it has come and gone, you cannot get it back. So it's extremely important to realize that you are a steward of this God-given time and must strive to use it wisely and to honor God. Think of your daily activities as fruit. The good and ripe fruits glorify God and maximize your efforts. The bad fruits, which cannot be eaten and must be discarded, are those futile habits that keep you from following God and fulfilling His purposes. These bitter and rotten fruits are "time robbers."

What time robbers are running and ruining your days? For starters, how about your phone? You don't always have to answer it. Another problem is interruptions. Learn to tell people you'll get back to them...and then set up a time that's convenient. Failing to delegate (even to your children at home) also wastes time. Unclear priorities mean you will probably try to move out in all directions at once rather than focus on the most important tasks.

What time robbers will you tackle today so you can manage your time and be more efficient and effective? As the Bible tells us in Colossians 1:10: "Walk worthy of the Lord, fully pleasing Him, being fruitful in every good work and increasing in the knowledge of God."

So teach us to number our days,
that we may present to You a heart of wisdom.
PSALM 90:12 NASB

Regret

*Dear Father in heaven, I thank You for the forgiveness
I experience each and every day in Jesus Christ.
Your forgiveness is a gift that I cherish and
humbly receive with utmost gratitude. I have sorrows,
sins, and regrets for my past and, bless You, Father,
that my sins were as scarlet, yet You have made them
as white as snow! Today I am asking for Your help to
remember those sins are truly forgiven by You and to
move forward into the sunshine of Your grace.
Thank You for the promise and reality of
Your forgiveness, that You forgive my sins and
remember them no more.*

Amen.

You are not alone in your struggle to live a godly life. Everyone's life is stained with sin and past regrets. But take heart! Jesus' death on the cross made God's forgiveness a reality. God described His forgiveness in this word picture when He said, "Though your sins are like scarlet, they shall be as white as snow; though they are red like crimson, they shall be as wool" (Isaiah 1:18).

Be assured that God loves you and cares for you. You can count on and enjoy the promise and reality of His forgiveness.

Forgiveness. Just the sound of the word brings joy and relief to the heart! In Jeremiah 31:34, God says, "I will forgive their iniquity." In fact, the verse goes on to say "and their sin I will remember no more." Claim that promise today and every day.

Don't brood over past situations and what has happened. Once you have talked a situation through with God and confessed any sin, you can move forward and make spiritual progress. There may be consequences from your past that you will have to deal with, but as you acknowledge your sin before God and receive His forgiveness, move on in serving Him and loving Him wholeheartedly with renewed joy. The apostle Paul had a dark past, and he could have wallowed in that past with overwhelming regrets, but hear now and remember what he chose to do instead:

> *Brethren, I do not count myself to have apprehended;*
> *but one thing I do, forgetting those things which are behind*
> *and reaching forward to those things which are ahead,*
> *I press toward the goal for the prize*
> *of the upward call of God in Christ Jesus.*
> PHILIPPIANS 3:13

Trusting God

*Father above, Your Word tells me to trust in You and
not lean on my own understanding. You promise that
as I acknowledge You, You will direct my path.
At times I have failed to trust You when circumstances
were difficult and overwhelming, but I am here
before You now to affirm my faith and trust in
Your promise! I know that I can trust You because
You have always provided for my needs.
And You have always guided me on Your path
when I looked to You for direction. So once again
I will step out in trust.
Thank You for supplying all my needs.*

Amen.

One of the greatest examples of someone who trusted God is Abraham of the Old Testament. We first meet this amazing man in Genesis 12:1 when he trusted God with his life, his family, and his future by departing from his lifelong home and going to an unknown region. He then trusted God's promise to provide an heir even in his old age. And in his most costly demonstration of trust, Abraham, when asked by God to sacrifice his long-awaited son, trusted that "God [would] provide for Himself the lamb for a burnt offering" (Genesis 22:8)—and God did! Abraham's trust in God was confirmed repeatedly.

Trusting God and His Word is at the core of the Christian faith. Do you trust the message of the gospel, that God sent Jesus to die for the sins of mankind, and that believing in Jesus, you are forgiven and will inherit eternal life? And do you trust God's promise that He "shall supply all your need" as stated in Philippians 4:19?

Whatever your challenge, your task, your trial, or your crisis, God will provide for you every step of the way. The wonderful fact is that when God commands You to do something, He will also enable you to obey. Step out in trust as you walk through your day with the Lord. Not a single day will go by without experiencing His care. God will help you meet your emotional, physical, mental, and spiritual challenges today and all your tomorrows.

Behold, God is my salvation,
I will trust and not be afraid;
"For YAH, the LORD, is my strength and song;
He also has become my salvation."

ISAIAH 12:2

The Future

*All-knowing Father, You know the beginning
from the end. I am exceedingly thankful and
greatly relieved that You are in control of all things.
As my heavenly Father, You hold my future in
Your hands. You know my heart, You also know
my dreams and desires. You know the plans
You have for me. And You promise to finish
the work You have begun in me! Help me,
O Lord of my life, to not be fearful of the future
but to trust You fully. The desire of my heart is
to follow You until I cross the finish line
and step into Your forever presence.*

Amen.

Sometimes it's impossible to sleep because we worry about what the future might hold. The future is the great unknown, and anything and everything is possible, including both good and evil. But God's Word assures us again and again that He is in complete control of all things. God's promise in Jeremiah 46:28 speaks for itself: "Do not fear...for I am with you." God is always at work in us and for us. No matter how severe or difficult we think our situation is, we can look forward with confidence.

God is faithful and powerful and always keeps His promises.

He will definitely do His part. And you must do your part by following the advice given in Philippians 4:8: "Whatever things are true...meditate on these things." The future is neither true nor real. You cannot manage or deal with what has not happened. Only the present is true and real, and you can rest and be at peace knowing the future is in God's hands, and trusting Him to do what is best for you. He will finish the work He has started in you (Philippians 1:6).

Look to God for strength to manage your present situation. Give yourself, your future, your relationships, and your work and responsibilities to God. You can exhale and relax in the truth that God has a perfect plan and purpose for your future. You can be at peace and live without doubt or fear. Nothing and no one can stop God's good work in you. That's His promise! As a woman after God's own heart, offer up heartfelt praise to God for this powerful promise to you:

I know the thoughts that I think toward you, says the LORD,
thoughts of peace and not of evil,
to give you a future and a hope.

JEREMIAH 29:11

Suffering

*Father, I admit I want to be free of pain and suffering.
But how could I hope to escape suffering when
Your only Son, God in flesh, the Lord Jesus Christ,
Messiah, suffered so much to pay for my sins?
Strengthen me to persevere when I am in a season
of suffering. And help me to look to You, Father,
and not lose hope, for I know You are watching over
me and will carry me through my times of distress.
Loving Father, thank You for Your faithful,
enabling love and care for me, Your grateful child.*

Amen.

Some Christians think that we are not meant to suffer, that God wants us to be free from the cares, concerns, and hardships of this life. Yet, the opposite is true. Jesus told His disciples they should expect to suffer. He said, "In the world you will have tribulation." Then Jesus shared the good news: "Be of good cheer, I have overcome the world" (John 16:33). Suffering is to be expected, but by His grace, our Lord Jesus will see us through whatever we are facing.

You may be going through a season of painful and difficult suffering today, but take a closer look around and you will discover that many are suffering even more than you. For example, in Jeremiah 52:31-34 we learn that King Jehoiachin of Judah was held captive in chains for 37 years! Jehoiachin's long season of suffering came to an end as the new king of Babylon released him and provided for Jehoiachin for the rest of his life.

Are you in a season of suffering? Whatever you do, keep on loving the Lord. Keep on praying and fulfilling His purposes, no matter how unclear, undesirable, or unexpected your circumstances are. Romans 5:3-5 reminds us that suffering produces spiritual growth: "We also glory in tribulations, knowing that tribulation produces perseverance; and perseverance, character; and character, hope. Now hope does not disappoint, because the love of God has been poured out in our hearts by the Holy Spirit who was given to us." Praise God for His love and for hope!

Beloved, do not think it strange
concerning the fiery trial which is to try you,
as though some strange thing happened to you;
but rejoice to the extent that you
partake of Christ's sufferings,
that when His glory is revealed,
you may also be glad with exceeding joy.

1 PETER 4:12-13

Daily Walk

*"Just a Closer Walk with Thee." God, today my
heartfelt prayer comes from this song that reminds me
of the importance of spending time with You.
I often stray from Your side and veer down the path of
my own self-will, but I want a closer walk with You
and a more intimate knowledge of You.
I look forward to talking with You daily in prayer
and learning more about You from Your Word.
As I draw closer to You, I know I will be blessed
with Your strength and guidance for all that comes
my way today. My prayer is, "Make me understand
the way of Your precepts; so shall I meditate on
Your wonderful works" (Psalm 119:27).*

Amen.

In the New Testament a close relationship with God is described as walking "in the Spirit" (Galatians 5:16). A daily walk with the Lord is not easy to sustain. In fact the apostle Paul described his challenge to walk with God as a battle: "We know that the law is spiritual, but I am carnal, sold under sin. For what I am doing, I do not understand. For what I will to do, that I do not practice; but what I hate, that I do" (Romans 7:14-15). How did Paul overcome this struggle? He wrote, "So then, with the mind I myself serve the law of God..." (verse 25).

You will always struggle in your daily walk with God, but a key essential of victory over that struggle is establishing a daily time with God. Many people think a quiet time with God doesn't matter. But it does—tremendously!

And don't forget to pray. God sees and hears you pray, and "the LORD is good to those who wait for Him, to the soul who seeks Him" (Lamentations 3:25). God uses your dedication to your walk with Him to teach you, guide you, and impart His wisdom. Be faithful to gear up for victorious living each day. Welcome God's efforts to prepare you to walk with Him through your next commitment, your next trial, your next hurdle, your next opportunity. Clear your calendar. Set aside time to place yourself before God. Sit in His presence. Take in His Word. Wait on Him. Then rise up and walk with Him.

Walk in the Spirit,
and you shall not fulfill the lust of the flesh...
If we live in the Spirit, let us also walk in the Spirit.
GALATIANS 5:16,25

Speech

*Lord, I did it again! I spoke to someone in a way that
was not edifying or helpful and has done great damage
to the other person and to our relationship.
I am miserable and humbly confess my sin.
I want to guard my thoughts and mouth,
and to speak words that honor You and build up others.
My prayer is that I will do as You say and lay aside
evil speaking and instead speak in love words that
comfort, help, and reflect
Your gracious presence in my life.*

Amen.

The Bible is filled with admonitions, cautions, and warnings about our speech. In the Old Testament, God specifically communicated He is against those who "have spoken nonsense and envisioned lies" (Ezekiel 13:8). God also said He hates "the perverse mouth" (Proverbs 8:13). In the New Testament we are told to lay aside "all malice, all deceit, hypocrisy, envy, and all evil speaking" (1 Peter 2:1). On the positive side, the Bible provides instruction and advice on speech that honors God. It tells us to "Let your speech always be with grace, seasoned with salt, that you may know how you ought to answer each one," and "Let no corrupt word proceed out of your mouth, but what is good for necessary edification, that it may impart grace to the hearers" (Colossians 4:6; Ephesians 4:29).

As a woman after God's own heart, you must choose to monitor your mouth. One good choice is to say nothing. But if you must speak, pray first and make the choice to control your tongue. Do as the Proverbs 31 woman did: "She opens her mouth with wisdom, and on her tongue is the law of kindness" (Proverbs 31:26).

I have never forgotten these words heard in a Sunday school class: "With every encounter, make it your aim that people are better off for having been in your presence. Try in every encounter to give something to the other person." You show your love for God by loving others with life-giving speech. Just for today, plan in every encounter to attempt to give something to the other person—a smile, a hug, a huge "hello," a word of encouragement, a compliment—that will better their day and their life in some way.

Let your speech always be with grace, seasoned with salt,
that you may know how you ought to answer each one.
COLOSSIANS 4:6

Worry

God of all comfort, I thank and praise You for Your presence in my life. Nothing is out of Your reach or beyond Your sight. Nothing happens in my life that You are not intimately involved in. Nothing can separate me from Your love and care. Therefore, Lord, there is nothing that I need to worry about! Thank You for the peace You give me that is beyond understanding. I rejoice in You!

Amen.

Worry is something most people—and women—love to do. And the things we worry about are as varied and numerous as all the issues and people in our lives and in our overactive imaginations. Whatever happens to be on our minds can spark a worry attack.

This response to our life situations, whether real or imaginary, is the 100 percent opposite response from God's instructions in His Word. Worry indicates a lack of trust in God's wisdom and His power. Worry will immobilize you. And worry will distract you from your worship and love of God.

The apostle Paul told believers how to win over the debilitating condition called worry. He began with a bold and comforting statement: "The Lord is at hand" (Philippians 4:5). Our Lord is always present with us, and it is His power that sustains us during times of deep concern. Therefore, there is no need to worry. Instead Paul says, "Be anxious for nothing" (Philippians 4:6). What should we do instead? "...In everything"—whatever we might want to worry about—"by prayer and supplication, with thanksgiving, let your requests be made known to God" (Philippians 4:6). Every difficulty and all problems are to be brought before God. What happens when we give our worries over to God? "The peace of God, which surpasses all understanding, will guard your hearts and minds through Christ Jesus" (verse 7).

The writer of Psalm 1:2 also had advice to help you counteract your anxious moments: "His delight is in the law of the LORD, and in His law he meditates day and night." Stay close to God through prayer and through His Word, and you will experience His peace. Then, of course, honor Him with genuine thanksgiving.

Worry does not empty tomorrow of its sorrows.
It empties today of its strength.
CORRIE TEN BOOM

Facing Your Fears

Father, You are unique in glory, honor, majesty,
and power. You are the one who spoke the universe
into existence. You are my shield and protector.
You have promised to protect me as a mother hen
protects her chicks under the safety of her wings.
I am embarking on a journey of hiding
Your promises in my heart so I will be less fearful.
Instead of cowering in fear, "whenever I am afraid,
I will trust in You" (Psalm 56:3), my Lord,
my Fortress, my Defender. I will focus on the truth that
You are with me always, anywhere, and everywhere.

Amen.

Fear is not a bad emotion. In fact, God has given us a mechanism many refer to as a "fight or flight" response. But for most of us, our fears and concerns are about the "what-ifs" in life. We are fearful of the unknown. Although nothing real is there to harm us, we are afraid of what we think might happen to us.

A sure way to face your fears is to equip yourself with the knowledge and assurance that comes from God's Word—from knowing His promises. In Deuteronomy 1:29-31, Moses reminded the people that because of God's faithfulness in the past, they could trust God for their future as they entered the Promised

Land: "Do not be terrified, or afraid of them. The LORD your God, who goes before you, He will fight for you." This instruction and powerful promise is repeated several more times in the book of Deuteronomy and throughout Scripture.

How do you overcome your fear of failure, of something new, of any number of things that might happen in the future? You cannot do anything about an uncertain future—that is in God's hands. But you can do something in the present that will prepare you for your unknown future. You can increase your knowledge of God and strengthen your faith in His Word and promises. This kind of wisdom and belief allows you to face your fears boldly with strength and endurance. Move out and move on. Conquer your fears. Follow God's instructions and do not be afraid. God is with you, and you can count on Him.

Whenever I am afraid,
I will trust in You.
In God (I will praise His word),
in God I have put my trust.
PSALM 56:3-4

Parenting

*God, I depend on You each day for wisdom and
energy and conviction as I raise my child.
Lord, I want to be a diligent student of Your Word
so I am a godly role model for my children.
And I want to be diligent to follow Your instructions to
teach them Your precepts. Help me to be an avid
prayer warrior on behalf of my children, praying
diligently and passionately for their salvation,
praying that they will walk faithfully in Your ways,
praying to be the parent You want me to be!
How I need Your help!*

Amen.

Any parent will tell you that raising children is one of life's greatest joys. They will also tell you it is a challenging and difficult undertaking. Parenting children at any age, whether a baby, a teen, or a young adult, is a huge responsibility which can be scary and confusing. The good news is that parents don't have to do it alone. Psalm 46:1 proclaims that "God is our refuge and strength."

Take comfort. God gives you direction, and His Word is always available to guide you each step of the way. Moses gave the children of Israel parenting instructions *before* they entered the Promised Land. Like Moses, your major task, and the one with eternal consequences, is to take every opportunity to impart God's precepts *before* they are needed, to "teach them diligently to your children, and…talk of them when you sit in your house, when you walk by the way, when you lie down, and when you rise up" (Deuteronomy 6:7).

Unfortunately, you cannot impart what you do not possess. Committing yourself and aiming at obedience to your heavenly Father will help you raise children who are obedient and possess the knowledge—and an example—they need to walk through this world and live according to God's Word. The apostle Paul said of his disciple Timothy, "From childhood you have known the Holy Scriptures, which are able to make you wise for salvation through faith which is in Christ Jesus" (2 Timothy 3:15). And moms and grandmoms, take notice. Timothy's mother and grandmother had devoted themselves to teaching young Timothy God's forever truths!

Your calling as a mother or grandmother is to faithfully live out what you know and believe in front of your children. Your careful, repeated instruction lays the groundwork in your child's heart to accept Jesus Christ as Savior.

Train up a child in the way he should go,
and when he is old he will not depart from it.
PROVERBS 22:6

Character

*God, all too often I measure myself against all
that the world promotes. I easily slip into thinking
I'm a nobody as I compare myself with other women.
I know that in Christ I am a new creation, and that
I am fearfully and wonderfully made—exactly the way
You meant for me to be. Today I am thinking on
my worth in You, knowing that I am beautiful in
Your eyes. Thank You for the many ways You encourage
my spiritual growth and reveal Your love for me.
Lord, I know I am precious in Your eyes, for You sent
Your Son to die for my sins, and I am eternally grateful!*

Amen.

Have you had days when you thought you must be invisible? It was as if you blended right into the background! Most every woman thinks this way at one time or another. This is when the world would say, "You need to bolster your self-image! You need to find yourself or develop a new identity." But these remarks and suggestions are not true for a Christian, especially when you understand God's view of you. Praise God, He tells you how you are to see yourself from His perspective and the response it should elicit. "I will give thanks to You, for I am fearfully and wonderfully made; wonderful are Your works, and my soul knows it very well" (Psalm 139:14 NASB). You are anything but invisible or average in God's eyes.

A woman who seeks her identity in Christ and considers Him as her lifelong traveling companion stands out. A godly woman is special because she keeps her word. She honors her vows. She nurtures her inner character—her inner beauty. She exhibits great faith in the Lord. She forges ahead in spite of any obstacles. And she positively affects her family, her community, and even the world!

Jot down the character qualities and godly traits you want in your life and begin actively pursuing them. Also read Proverbs 31:10-31 for more ideas. You will be blessed by the many qualities in this woman of excellence! Then use your list as your prayer list, and don't be surprised when God moves you from the ordinary to the extraordinary!

Charm is deceitful and beauty is passing,
but a woman who fears the LORD,
she shall be praised.
PROVERBS 31:30

Family

Father of all mankind, You created the first family
when You created Adam and Eve. My family is
important to You and should be to me as well.
I thank You for my parents who have guided me
over the years, and now, O Lord, give me the grace
and strength to be available for them.
And thank You too for my husband and his family.
Help me work on deepening these all-important
family relationships. I am also asking You to
help me teach and model for my children
the importance of family. And Father,
I thank You that I am a member of
the family of God!

Amen.

It cannot be expressed too strongly that family is your number one priority after your incredible relationship with God. He designed the family to be the glue that holds society together, and it is the first place the enemy attacks. Think about your relationships with your parents and family and your in-laws. First, if you are married, loving your family starts with your husband. When you deliberately choose to focus your love and attention on him, all of your other family relationships will fall into place.

The Bible contains instruction about the respect and honor God wants you to extend to your husband (Ephesians 5:22,33). And many scriptures communicate you are to "'honor your father and mother,' which is the first commandment with promise: 'that it may be well with you and you may live long on the earth'" (Ephesians 6:2-3; see also Exodus 20:12; Deuteronomy 27:16). Even though you are an adult and may also have a family of your own, you are still to love, respect, and honor your parents and in-laws. It is not optional—it is a command.

As you mature spiritually, God provides all of the grace and character resources you need to get along with anyone, including your family members, parents, and in-laws. Ask yourself often, and especially when you are struggling, "How do I want my children to treat me when they are adults?" Then realize that right now you are modeling to your children how they should treat you and their future relatives.

There is no more consistent, pregnant, dynamic forum
for instruction about life than the family,
because that is exactly what God designed the family to be,
a learning community.
PASTOR PAUL DAVID TRIPP

Comfort

*God of all comfort, You know what I face each day,
and I am clinging to Your instruction to "be anxious
for nothing." When I am troubled, I will remember
and count on Your presence. Open my heart to
Your counsel and Your comfort today. May I know
Your peace in my circumstances. Grant me patience
when my heart is restless. And guide me with
the light of Your hope through this journey.
I bless and praise You for Your care and
Your comfort.*

Amen.

Do you have an ongoing burden? Others may sympathize, give comfort, and try to help, but even then, you may feel like you are alone as you experience the hardships you must endure. When you catch yourself thinking you are alone in your daily trials, know that you are never alone. Deuteronomy 33:27 assures you "the eternal God is your refuge, and underneath are the everlasting arms." Isn't it a comfort to know that your life, with its ongoing struggles, is covered and carried by the Lord? He is with you every step of the way. And He will enable you to walk through the valley of the shadow of death when the time arrives (Psalm 23:4).

God will not falter when it comes to keeping His promises of care and protection. Numbers 23:19 reminds us of the constant character of God: "God is not a man, that He should lie, nor a son of man, that He should repent. Has He said, and will He not do? Or has He spoken, and will He not make it good?"

Know that the Lord is beside you to give you comfort and to guide you. And as you give Him the weight of your every fear, worry, pain, and heartache, you will experience "the peace of God, which surpasses all understanding" which will guard your heart and mind "through Christ Jesus" (Philippians 4:7).

So keep on walking. Keep on enduring, just for today. Keep on keeping on! Then tomorrow get up and wait patiently on the Lord. He hears your cries. He knows your struggles. He keeps His promises. And He will extend to you His strength and comfort for one more day. Because of His enduring love, you can endure!

Blessed be the God and Father of our Lord Jesus Christ,
the Father of mercies and God of all comfort,
who comforts us in all our tribulation.
2 CORINTHIANS 1:3-4

Success

God, You told Your servant Joshua that if he would meditate day and night on Your Word and follow what was written there, You would give him success. Lord, I desire more than anything to please You. I want to be a success in Your eyes. Open my heart to devour Your Word so I can discern and discover Your will. Strengthen me to step out on the path to greater faith and faithfulness so I can better live out Your plan. Lead me in the path You choose. Then I truly will be on the path to success!

Amen.

Where does God have you today? What responsibilities have been given to you by the Lord? And what's happening to your dreams and your heart's desires? Many of these activities and desires indicate God's directions for your life. Be sure you set aside some time to discover what the Bible says about your roles as a woman and to pray about them.

God's road to success is quite simple: As you faithfully follow Him with all your heart, soul, mind, and strength, and are obedient to seek His will, you will be blessed and enjoy success. Consider King David, who was in a difficult situation during a war. What did David do? "David inquired of the LORD..." When the king sought God's guidance, God answered, "Go up, for I will doubtless deliver the Philistines into your hand" (2 Samuel 5:19). The road to God's brand of success requires you to do as David did and seek God's guidance minute by minute throughout your day as you must make decision after decision.

Yes, you are human, and you will definitely have moments when you fail. But as you get up and dust yourself off, look to God. Rely on Him and do what He asks of you through His Word and in answer to your prayers. Then you will be "successful" in His eyes, and that's all the success you need!

This Book of the Law shall not depart from your mouth,
but you shall meditate in it day and night,
that you may observe to do according to
all that is written in it.
For then you will make your way prosperous,
and then you will have good success.

JOSHUA 1:8

Inner Strength

*Dear Shepherd of my soul, there is so much pain and
suffering in this world, and it has touched my life too.
My emotions are high...and my energy is low.
Yet, as my great Shepherd, You are the restorer of my soul.
Today I come to You with great expectation,
knowing that You can and will refill my empty heart
and restore the joy of my salvation. You, the almighty
God of the universe, are the only One who can give me
strength to endure. You are the only One who can renew
my spirit so I can keep on keeping on—
no matter what I am facing today
or will face in the future.*

Amen.

How do we go on when tragedy strikes? The death of a loved one, divorce, infertility, betrayal, a cancer diagnosis, and more are all extremely difficult situations. How do we handle what life brings our way?

In 2 Samuel 12:20 we see how King David responded to the death of his infant son: "So David arose from the ground, washed and anointed himself, and changed his clothes; and he went into the house of the LORD and worshiped." Worship was this heartbroken father's response to loss, and it should be ours as well. David went to the great Shepherd for strength. Let these four words in Psalm 23:3, which were written by David, speak to your heartaches: "He restores my soul." Your wonderful Lord not only takes care of your physical needs, but He also takes care of your spiritual needs.

Whatever your grievous situation, you can have hope because you have a mighty and compassionate and loving God who can and will restore your soul. God will come to the rescue. His tender care, along with His promises to heal, strengthen, and restore you, will tend to your broken heart.

Don't wait for tragedy to strike before you seek God's help. "Wait on the Lord" right now. Meet with Him daily through His Word. Draw closer to the Father through prayer so you are strong spiritually when tragedy strikes—and it will! And walk closely to the good Shepherd, drawing strength from Him. You will be able to rise up in God's strength and fortitude, ready to face and manage tragedy. Praise be to God!

For the LORD *has comforted His people*
and will have compassion on His afflicted.
ISAIAH 49:13 NASB

Hurting

Lord Jesus, I know You identify with my hurt and pain.
You, the spotless Son of God, who did no sin,
were betrayed, beaten, and killed. And yet, Lord,
while dying on the cross You prayed for the Father
to forgive Your tormentors. Dear Lord, my tears are
flowing as I struggle to find the words to pray as
I am hurting. Turn my mourning into joy and
clothe me with gladness (Psalm 30:11).
Give me strength to follow Your example and
forgive those who have hurt me.
Hold me, Lord. I am trusting in You.

Amen.

You probably know scores of women who have been hurt in many ways by others. They say things like, "I thought we'd grow old together. Where did I miss the signals?" "What did or didn't I do for this to happen?" "Why did a woman I considered to be a friend turn on me and desert me in my hour of need?"

This may have been how the apostle Paul felt as he described the defection of one of his key disciples: "Be diligent to come to me quickly; for Demas has forsaken me, having loved this present world, and has departed..." (2 Timothy 4:9-10). The word "forsaken" means to leave someone uncared for—to leave someone in a grievous situation.

You may be a hurting woman today who is trying to answer these and numerous other unanswerable questions about hurts you have experienced. You may be crying out with words similar to these words of Scripture: "Has God forgotten to be gracious? Has He in anger shut up His tender mercies?" (Psalm 77:9).

Unfortunately, in our sinful world people hurt people. Family members hurt family members. And even God's people hurt each other. The list goes on. When you wrestle with despair, when all seems hopeless, put your God-given faith to work and trust in the Lord. And no, God has not forgotten you...and never will. Believe that God will sustain you today and all the days of your life, in whatever burdens you are experiencing. Note below how Paul responded to being hurt and disappointed by those around him. Make these words your prayer and praise as well.

But the Lord stood with me and strengthened me...
And the Lord will deliver me from every evil work
and preserve me for His heavenly kingdom.
To Him be glory forever and ever. Amen!
2 TIMOTHY 4:17-18

Time with God

God, as the author of all revelation, I thank You that You have revealed Yourself to me through Your Son, the living Word, the Lord Jesus, and also through Your written Word, the Bible. As I read and absorb Your written Word, I better understand how marvelous Your works are and the future You have planned for me. By Your grace I want to dedicate more time every day to learning about You. Help me deal with distractions that come along and derail my time with You. I want to isolate myself for some much-needed quiet time each day so I can focus more fully on You, my wonderful Lord.

Amen.

How special is God's Word to you? Do you consider the Bible to be a book for casual reading which you tuck under your arm when you go to church and put back on its shelf at home until next week? This is not how Job described his devotion to God's Word. He testified, "I have treasured the words of His mouth more than my necessary food" (Job 23:12).

Do you need guidance? God's Word has all the guidance you will ever need: "Your word is a lamp to my feet and a light to my path" (Psalm 119:105). And how about temptation? Again God's

Word gives you the solution: "Your word I have hidden in my heart, that I might not sin against You" (Psalm 119:11).

Whenever you feel like "I've tried, but reading my Bible and praying every day is not possible with my schedule," open your eyes and your heart and give Bible and prayer time another try. You will immediately notice a difference. You will see that being in God's Word on a daily basis is as necessary as eating and breathing. These keys can help you strengthen the discipline of Bible study and prayer:

- ～ Refuse to miss a day in God's Word. It is at the heart of every woman who loves God, even a busy woman like you.

- ～ Ask God to open your eyes and heart to His truths.

- ～ Make yourself accountable to Christian friends or find a faithful pray er partner.

- ～ Get up early before everyone makes demands on your time.

- ～ Remember something is better than nothing, and...

- ～ Always aim for more!

Pray these words from God's Word as you begin your devotional time:

Open my eyes, that I may see
wondrous things from Your law.
PSALM 119:18

Confession

*Father God, You are too pure to look on sin and iniquity.
I come to You now using David's prayer of confession
as my own: "I acknowledge my transgressions,
and my sin is always before me. Against You,
You only, have I sinned, and done this evil in
Your sight" (Psalm 51:3-4). I realize that even
my slightest transgression is wrong in light of
Your holiness. Help me to quickly confess my sin and
my pride to You. Lead me to seek forgiveness
from You and from others—so I may have
sweet fellowship with You, walk with You,
and serve You. Thank You for the forgiveness I receive
in Jesus, Your Son and my Lord and Savior.*

Amen.

One of the first things God did after the children of Israel completed the tabernacle in the wilderness was teach the people how to handle their sin. God said, "When a man or woman commits any sin that men commit in unfaithfulness against the LORD, and that person is guilty, then he shall confess the sin..." (Numbers 5:6-7). Furthermore, all sin committed against another person was considered a sin against God Himself. That's why David considered his adulterous and murderous sins against Bathsheba and Uriah as sins against God. David prayed, "Against You, You only, have I sinned, and done this evil in Your sight..." (Psalm 51:4).

How do you handle your sin? Are you stubborn? Prideful? Do you stand your ground even when you are wrong? It's hard to admit failure, and it's embarrassing! But God tells His people to confess and admit their sins, to seek Him in prayer, and ask Him for forgiveness. The result? The condition of your situation—and your heart—and even your physical state will greatly improve.

In Psalm 32:4-5 David expressed the incredible benefits of confessing sin: "Day and night Your hand was heavy upon me; my vitality was turned into the drought of summer. I acknowledged my sin to You, and my iniquity I have not hidden. I said, 'I will confess my transgressions to the LORD,' and You forgave the iniquity of my sin." You will slip up again and again, but remember to use each sin as an opportunity to grow closer to God.

Have mercy upon me, O God,
according to Your lovingkindness;
according to the multitude of Your tender mercies,
blot out my transgressions.
Wash me thoroughly from my iniquity,
and cleanse me from my sin.

PSALM 51:1-2

Obedience

Righteous Father, I confess there are times
when I want to do my own thing in my own way,
to indulge myself and not listen to anyone else—
sometimes even You! Lord, not only are You faithful
to forgive my disobedience, but You also extend
Your grace to me when I fail to live up to
Your standards. I want to be a woman after
Your own heart, a woman who will do all
Your will. I ask for Your forgiveness...
and Your patience and love! I love You and
want to be obedient to do what
Your Word says—to do Your will.

Amen.

How can you become a woman after God's own heart? By being a woman "who will do all [God's] will" (Acts 13:22). Obedience is the expression of a heart that loves God. In fact, God desires obedience above religious activity. Hear what the prophet Samuel told the disobedient King Saul: "Has the Lord as great delight in burnt offerings and sacrifices, as in obeying the voice of the Lord? Behold, to obey is better than sacrifice, and to heed than the fat of rams" (1 Samuel 15:22).

Obedience to God and His Word will place you in the center

of His will. To do this, determine that the split second you think or do anything you know displeases God, you will stop immediately. This action will train your heart to be responsive to God in your daily trials, temptations, and situations. If you gossip—stop. If you think unworthy thoughts—stop. If you have a spark of anger—stop before you act on it.

Everyone has experiences like these. But it's up to you how you will respond, and your response will reveal what is at the core of your heart. Remember, delayed obedience is really disobedience. So call on the Lord right away. Immediately. As soon as possible. As 1 John 1:9 promises, God is "faithful and just to forgive us our sins and to cleanse us from all unrighteousness." Here are a few more "favorite sins" you can tackle:

Put off all these: anger, wrath, malice,
blasphemy, filthy language out of your mouth.
Do not lie to one another.

COLOSSIANS 3:8-9

Let all bitterness, wrath, anger, clamor, and evil speaking
be put away from you, with all malice.
And be kind to one another, tenderhearted,
forgiving one another,
even as God in Christ forgave you.

EPHESIANS 4:31-32

Ministry

*Lord God, in the past You set aside a special group
of people to minister before You in the temple.
Today You have gifted and tasked each of your
people—including me—to minister to
fellow believers. Thank You for the life experiences
You have given me, all of which could be helpful
to others. You have filled my life with meaning,
and my heart overflows with thanksgiving.
Now, Father, help me to press on in serving others
in order to bring them more of Your Word,
Your wisdom, and the knowledge of You,
the source of real life.*

Amen.

You have probably heard this comment: "I've had my time of ministry. I've done my duty. It's time for others to take over and minister in the church. Let some of the younger people do their time in ministry." In the Old Testament this was true. Priests and Levites had age restrictions on their service. But this is not true for believers today in the church age. First Corinthians 12:7 explains, "The manifestation of the Spirit is given to each one for the profit of all." When it comes to serving the Lord, there is no "season" for service and no age limit. It's true there are indeed "seasons" in our roles, responsibilities, and life, but the service to God's people can continue indefinitely.

In the same way that God gifted the priests in Numbers 18:7, God has given every believer gifts for ministry. Serving others is ageless and ongoing. In Philippians 3:14, the apostle Paul, who was well into his sixties, shared that he continued to "press toward the goal for the prize of the upward call of God in Christ Jesus."

As long as you have life and breath, you are called to serve others...to press on. And, like Paul, the older you get, the more meaningful and fulfilling your ministry can be. Your years in the Lord give you greater experience, greater knowledge of God's Word, greater wisdom, greater faith, and sometimes greater amounts of time. Even with your dying breath, you can still be praying for people in your family, your church, and on the mission field. So plan, prepare, practice, and pray, and by God's grace, proceed forward toward a lifetime of ministry.

Having then gifts differing
according to the grace that is given to us,
let us use them:
if...ministry, let us use it in our ministering.
ROMANS 12:6-7

Thinking on the Truth

*Lord, You are the God who heals, and I need
a major change in the area of my thoughts. Too often
I spiral down into the dark tunnel of negative thinking.
I become depressed, sorrowful, bitter, and resentful.
Thank You for the brilliant truths that come to my
rescue when I read and meditate on Your Word.
You have showered me with so many
magnificent blessings, and I want to focus on
thinking on these positive and life-changing gifts.
Most of all I want to saturate my mind with
facts and truths about You, Lord.
Help me renew my mind according to Your Word.*

Amen.

Are you constantly thinking negative thoughts? Do you second-guess what others say? Do your thoughts lead you to anger or depression or other destructive emotions? Being a woman after God's own heart is all about "minding your mind" and "thinking on the truth." To live out God's plan for your busy life with passion and purpose, you must harness the ten-thousand-plus thoughts that pass through your mind each day. Your mind must be disciplined for God's purposes and for His glory. That is a tall challenge!

Praise God, His Word comes to our rescue. The apostle Paul shared this encouraging truth: "Now may our Lord Jesus Christ Himself...who has loved us and given us everlasting consolation...comfort your hearts" (2 Thessalonians 2:16-17). One way the Lord comforts your heart is by reminding you again and again of Philippians 4:8, which instructs, "...whatever things are true, whatever things are noble, whatever things are just, whatever things are pure, whatever things are lovely, whatever things are of good report, if there is any virtue and if there is anything praiseworthy—meditate on these things."

You can and must shift your focus away from negative thinking and onto God instead. You can train yourself to dwell on what is true and real. As you harness your thoughts so they match those named in Philippians 4:8, you can turn your attention onto God and His faithfulness, and trust Him to carry you through. Choose to enjoy the peace of mind that is yours when you think on what is true and real.

I will meditate on the glorious splendor of Your majesty,
and on Your wondrous works.

PSALM 145:5

Spiritual Gifts

Father, I thank and praise You for sending Your Spirit to indwell me and empower me with Your gifts of the Spirit for service to Your people. You have made me and uniquely prepared me for ministry with a special set of gifts You have granted to me. It humbles me to even think that I could help others. Please lead me to discover and determine my giftedness. I want to devote myself to nurturing my gifts and using them to benefit Your people in the body of Christ.

Amen.

It is hard to imagine that the God of the universe wants to have a personal relationship with those who accept His Son as Lord and Savior. But that is exactly what God has done. Along with that personal relationship, God has given you a personalized set of abilities, which are referred to as "the manifestation of the Spirit" (1 Corinthians 12:7).

This truth answers the question, "Do I have a spiritual gift or gifts?" First Corinthians 12 describes their function: "The manifestation of the Spirit is given to each one for the profit of all..." (see verses 4,7-9).

Yes, as a believer you have spiritual gifts. The activity or process of discovering, developing, and using your mixture of gifts brings joy. So, what do you enjoy doing for others? Another attribute of spiritual gifts is that your service blesses others and you. Your gifts will also create opportunities for repeat service. God has given you your spiritual giftedness as a stewardship, and the church suffers when its people don't develop and use their gifts. Please don't miss out on the joy of bettering the lives of others in the body of Christ by not using your spiritual gifts.

If you are unsure about how to identify and use your spiritual gifts, here's a way to get started. Serving, showing mercy, and giving are three of the spiritual gifts listed in Romans 12:7-8. However, these same three spiritual gifts are commanded of every Christian and modeled for us by our dear Savior, in whose steps we are to follow. So commit now and begin to serve, show mercy, and give—and thus fulfill the law of God and encourage His people.

As each one has received a gift,
minister it to one another,
as good stewards of the manifold grace of God.
1 PETER 4:10

Attitude

Lord, Your Word tells me to rejoice always,
to be thankful for all things, to be gracious, kind,
humble, and a servant to all. I come before You today
acknowledging that too often I fail to exhibit
an attitude that honors You and gives the world
an accurate picture of what a transformed life looks like.
I am painfully aware of what it means to have
a bad attitude! With Your help, I want to embrace a
consistant attitude that reflects You and Your gospel of love.
I want to walk humbly as one
who loves and serves others.

Amen.

Attitude is everything. Why? Because your actions, which are the result of your attitudes, are a reflection of what's in your heart. What did God say to Cain right before he killed his brother Abel? "Why are you angry? And why has your countenance fallen?" (Genesis 4:6). In other words, "Cain, why do you have a bad attitude?" Cain's attitude reflected a murderous heart that resulted in murdering his brother! That is why the Bible cautions us to "keep your heart with all diligence, for out of it spring the issues of life" (Proverbs 4:23).

As a Christian, your attitudes toward others, your work, and your daily life reflect your heart attitude toward God. God asks you to be joyful, agreeable, hospitable, thankful, kind, and gracious to all. He asks you to do your work with enthusiasm. He asks that you serve your family and your employer wholeheartedly, that you treat those you interact with throughout the day with respect. Petition God in prayer for an obedient heart and an attitude of gratitude. Your faithfulness to God's direction is noticed by others, blesses others, and points others to Jesus Christ. Are people getting an accurate picture of Jesus from your life?

Second Corinthians 3:3 says, "Clearly you are an epistle of Christ, ministered by us, written not with ink but by the Spirit of the living God, not on tablets of stone but on tablets of flesh, that is, of the heart." This verse is a divine reminder to live in a manner that reflects Jesus Christ in us—a gospel read by all. So, what is the gospel according to you?

A good man out of the good treasure of his heart
brings forth good things,
and an evil man out of the evil treasure
brings forth evil things.
MATTHEW 12:35

Love

*Merciful God of love, with a heart filled with gratitude
I acknowledge and praise You that You love me
unconditionally and with an everlasting love.
Thankfully, Your love for me is not based on my actions
and attitudes. Your love sent Your only Son to die for
my sins. You have shown me love, and that love
shows me how to share Your love with others,
especially with my family and friends.
Now, Father of love, I ask for Your help in
loving those who are difficult to love. By Your grace,
I want to love these and all people with Your love.*

Amen.

The Bible calls us to love. In 1 John 4:7 we read, "Beloved, let us love one another, for love is of God; and everyone who loves is born of God and knows God."

And Jesus calls us to love saying, "You shall love your neighbor as yourself" (Matthew 22:39). You have probably heard this "golden rule" a thousand times while you were growing up. But putting the command to "love one another" (John 13:34) into action is a real challenge. Christ's call to "love your neighbor as yourself" goes one step further: "Let us not love in word or in tongue, but in deed and in truth" (1 John 3:18). You make your love evident to others by what you say and how you act. True love is an action. It does not pretend. It is for real. It has no ulterior motives and willingly gives, expecting nothing in return.

Is there any person who is not receiving your sincere love? God is calling you to love that person, no matter what. It's easy to talk about loving God, but loving others is another story! Like the saying goes, "Oh, we love God. We just hate people!" Your love for others reveals how much you truly love God. How are you measuring up? As you read God's definition of love below, are there any changes you must make to "love one another"?

Love suffers long and is kind; love does not envy;
love does not parade itself, is not puffed up;
does not behave rudely, does not seek its own,
is not provoked, thinks no evil;
does not rejoice in iniquity, but rejoices in the truth;
bears all things, believes all things,
hopes all things, endures all things.
Love never fails.

1 CORINTHIANS 13:4-8

Sharing the Good News!

Just before Jesus returned to heaven, He gave this command, "You shall be witnesses to Me in Jerusalem, and in all Judea and Samaria, and to the end of the earth" (Acts 1:8). This command to be His witnesses has never changed. Today you are to be a witness of the saving grace of Jesus to a lost world. Sharing your faith can be a scary thing, especially when talking to a complete stranger!

But a more natural way, especially for women, is to share your testimony casually through friendships and associations with neighbors and workmates. This is what Jesus encouraged the demon-possessed man to do after he had been healed of his demons. The man wanted to stay with Jesus, but Jesus told him, "'Return to your own house, and tell what great things God has done for you.' And he went his way and proclaimed throughout the whole city what great things Jesus had done for him" (Luke 8:39).

You are on a mission for God to tell others "what great things God has done for you." You don't need to memorize verses, though this would be helpful. Just be yourself. And like the blind man who was healed by Jesus, you can simply say, "One thing I know: that though I was blind, now I see" (John 9:25). Give the good news of the gospel to the people God brings your way. Share with them the hope of eternal life through Jesus Christ. Show them what a transformed life looks like. Give them a living example of what it means to be a woman after God's own heart—a woman saved by His grace.

I am not ashamed of the gospel of Christ,
for it is the power of God
to salvation for everyone who believes.

ROMANS 1:16

Serving Others

Father God, how I thank You for the gift of Your Son,
the Lord Jesus Christ. He was God in human flesh,
yet He was the greatest servant who ever lived!
He said that He "did not come to be served,
but to serve" (Mark 10:45). I need to be more
like Jesus, who stopped to minister to suffering people
no matter how busy He was. Today as I seek to follow in
Jesus' steps of humble, loving service, open my eyes to
opportunities around me to serve others...as He did.

Amen.

Meet Mary Magdalene, Joanna, Susanna, Salome, and Mary, the mother of James—a lovely, dedicated, courageous group of faithful women who used their time, money, and resources to serve Jesus and His disciples on their preaching tours (Luke 8:2-3). They even served Him in death as they prepared spices for His burial (Mark 16:1). How simple and yet how incredibly meaningful is that?

Dorcas was another woman who had a servant's heart. The Bible says she was "full of good works and charitable deeds" (Acts 9:36). This thoughtful lady noticed that the widows needed clothes, so she acted and made clothes for them.

Use whatever resources and talents you have to help and serve others. Every meal prepared, every piece of clothing washed, every room tidied, every shut-in visited, every act of doing something for others is love in action. There is no better time than the present to notice other people's needs and do something about them. Ask God to lead you to people who need encouragement, support, and prayer. Notice those around you and keep a keen eye out for ways you can help. Watch, listen, pray, and respond! Married or single, you can exercise your servant heart wherever you are.

Tape this over your kitchen sink or on the refrigerator door or at your desk: "True service is love in working clothes." Put on the work clothes of love and serve others, beginning right under your own roof. You can accomplish great things when you act on God's instructions. You don't have to wait for more experience, more education, more money. You can start serving the Lord today. Ask God to make your heart a servant's heart.

If anyone serves Me, let him follow Me;
and where I am, there My servant will be also.
If anyone serves Me, him My Father will honor.
JOHN 12:26

Fear of Death

*Dear Father, Your Son, the Lord Jesus Christ,
was raised from the dead, and I thank You that I too
have been raised in newness of life everlasting.
Therefore, I will not fear physical death,
as it is only the gateway to eternal life forever in
Your presence. Until that day may I approach and
live out each day as Your servant Paul did:
"To me, to live is Christ, and to die is gain."
With this confidence, I can boldly live this day
with joy and rejoicing.*

Amen.

Most everyone has a lingering fear of death. Death is the great unknown and the world views death with great fear. It is true that every person is going to die. This may sound harsh and callous, but it is a fact of life.

How are you handling this fact of life? Do you wake up most days fearful of death? Do you go to any and every extreme hoping and praying to delay the inevitable? If you are a believer in Christ, you are to take care of your physical body, but beyond that, you should adopt Paul's perspective: "To me, to live is Christ, and to die is gain" (Philippians 1:21). For Paul, Christ was his reason for living. Death would merely relieve him of his earthly burdens and allow him to fully worship and glorify Christ in heaven. As Jesus promised, "I go and prepare a place for you...[and] I will come again and receive you to Myself; that where I am, there you may be also" (John 14:2-3).

All believers will experience physical death, but not spiritual death. At the moment of salvation you were declared righteous before God. And as Romans 8:1 says, "There is therefore now no condemnation to those who are in Christ Jesus." Because you are in Christ, you have no reason to fear death. So make the most of the time you have. Witness to those who don't know Christ. Love your family and serve God and His people. Enjoy your life in Christ to the max while here on earth, and look forward with anticipation to the blessing of eternal life that is waiting for you in heaven.

"O Death, where is your sting?
O Hades, where is your victory?"
...But thanks be to God, who gives us the victory
through our Lord Jesus Christ.
1 CORINTHIANS 15:55-57

Guidance

*You, O God, are the great Shepherd of Your sheep.
I thank You that You guide me beside still waters.
You guide me in the path of righteousness.
And ultimately You will guide me to my eternal home
with You in heaven. Father, it grieves me when I rush
into my day angry, frustrated, and irritable because
I didn't begin my day asking You for Your guidance.
I know this behavior is not pleasing to You.
And I know it does not minister to
my family, friends, and coworkers.
Let Your words of Scripture refresh and
revive my heart and soul today.
May Your powerful Word encourage me and
guide me to every good work.*

Amen.

Would you ever think of starting a journey into an uncharted area or unfamiliar wilderness without a guide? No, of course not. But that's exactly what you are doing when you start your days without consulting with God through prayer and His Word. This one discipline of seeking God's guidance will set the focus for the hours that make up your day. Even a few minutes alone with God will transform your busy day from chaos to order and from panic to peace. This simple beginning will dramatically alter the events and the quality of your day. That's the promise of Proverbs 3:5-6: "Trust in the LORD with all your heart, and lean not on your own understanding; in all your ways acknowledge Him, and He shall direct your paths." Yet another proverb amplifies this truth: "The commandment is a lamp, and the law a light" (Proverbs 6:23).

Reading God's Word changes your thinking, your choices, and your behavior. The Bible is a tool the Holy Spirit uses to inform, teach, encourage, and guide you in the way you should live each day. Before you step into your busy day (which is *God's* day), spend time in God's Word. As you read His Word and set your mind on things above, you will be calm, steady, and focused as God guides you and leads the way. Because you started your day with Him, no matter what happens, you will be ready to tackle your day's work and any problems that arise—God's way.

The LORD is my shepherd; I shall not want.
He makes me to lie down in green pastures;
He leads me beside the still waters...
He leads me in the paths of righteousness
for His name's sake.

PSALM 23:1-3

Perseverance

*God of all patience, You want and expect me to
be patient and wait on Your leading.
Sometimes this is hard, and I strike out on my own,
which is usually a horrible mistake. Thank You for
not giving up on me and for forgiving my waywardness.
I want to follow You and persevere, to be steadfast.
Show me the way. Direct me to go on and on in
Your grace and to keep up a forward-moving pace.
I will look to You and rely on Your strength to
go the distance, to keep the faith,
and to finish the race.*

Amen.

In 2 Timothy 4:7, Paul compared the Christian life to a race. He declared, "I have fought the good fight, I have finished the race, I have kept the faith." Indeed it would be wonderful to be able to make such a statement at the end of your days on earth: "I have kept my faith."

The Christian life is not a sprint to the finish line. No, it is a long-distance race, like running a marathon of 26 miles, 385 yards or 42.195 kilometers...and more! Your Christian life is to be one of prolonged obedience in the same direction. To complete this noble task requires an extraordinary dose of perseverance so it may be said of you: "Here is the patience of the saints; here are those who keep the commandments of God and the faith of Jesus" (Revelation 14:12).

Running and finishing the race toward the goal of our high calling in Christ is something that requires discipline of body, life, and soul. Isaiah 40:31 says that "those who wait on the LORD...shall mount up with wings like eagles...shall run and not be weary...shall walk and not faint."

Be a woman who waits on the Lord. Consult God so you don't waste time and energy by riding off in all directions at once. God has a single destination in mind for your race—heaven, and He wants you to be patient, persistent, and persevering, praying always for strength and guidance. When you do this, you will run with perseverance. You will walk with confidence. And God will bless you with His strength for the race.

Let us lay aside every weight,
and the sin which so easily ensnares us,
and let us run with endurance
the race that is set before us,
looking unto Jesus.

HEBREWS 12:1-2

Money

*Father, all that I have has come from You,
and I thank You for all that I have—and don't have!
Keep me from loving money and wanting more and
more and more! Help me to guard my heart from
greed and ungratefulness. Please show me the
best ways to use what I have, and teach me to
be more careful, compassionate, and generous.
I want to be a good steward of every gift that comes
from Your hand. Thank You for those gifts.*

Amen.

Whether you have a lot of money or very little, you can easily let money take over your thoughts and priorities. But more important things than money deserve your time and focus. For instance, character. Your reputation is a higher priority than money. Humility is better than money. And wisdom is more desirable than gold.

In Luke 16:13, Jesus taught, "No servant can serve two masters; for either he will hate the one and love the other, or else he will be loyal to the one and despise the other. You cannot serve God and mammon." And "mammon" (meaning money) is a cruel master! Money itself is not evil. But as with many things in life, money management is a matter of the heart. "The love of money is a root of all kinds of evil" (1 Timothy 6:10). Whether you have a lot or a little is not the issue. It's how you manage it that counts, and "the love of money" will warp how you manage and use it. When God is your master, the amount of money you have takes a backseat.

As Christians, we are warned to beware of the "deceitfulness of riches, and the desires for other things" (Mark 4:19). First Timothy 6:18 gets to the heart of a godly woman's purposes: "Be rich in good works, ready to give, willing to share." Management of the money and possessions God entrusts to you is a spiritual issue and requires spiritual discipline and character. Honor the Lord with your possessions and with your money. After all, it all came from Him.

Money never stays with me.
It would burn me if it did.
I throw it out of my hands as soon as possible,
lest it should find its way into my heart.
JOHN WESLEY

Bitterness

Father God, with His dying breath
Your Son asked You to forgive those who crucified Him.
Another man, Stephen, asked You to forgive
those who were stoning him to death.
Your Word tells me to forgive as many times as
I have been sinned against—and more.
I don't want bitterness to hinder my relationship
with You, my loving and forgiving Lord.
I am coming before You today, begging for Your help
to be a woman who forgives even when
it's hard and it hurts—a woman who forgives
just as I have been forgiven. Thank You
for my salvation and Your forgiveness.

Amen.

The one prevalent human response to pain is to become resentful and bitter, either toward the person or persons who hurt us, or toward God, or both! Bitterness against someone who has wronged you is an evil cancer that, left unchecked, can destroy you. The Bible tells us to put away bitterness (Ephesians 4:31), "looking carefully...lest any root of bitterness springing up cause trouble, and by this many become defiled" (Hebrews 12:15).

The antidote to bitterness is forgiveness. As Jesus hung on the cross, He prayed, "Father, forgive them, for they do not know what they do" (Luke 23:34). Stephen followed his Lord's example and cried out, "Lord, do not charge them with this sin," as a mob continued stoning him to death (Acts 7:60).

When you fail to forgive others, you sentence yourself to a life of bitterness. Helen Roseveare was a missionary doctor who was brutally assaulted while serving in Africa. Yet, by God's grace, she forgave those who wronged her and spent 20 more years doing missionary service. Forgiving her abusers freed her to continue her mission of serving others. Another outstanding woman of faith, Elisabeth Elliot, forgave the men who savagely killed her missionary husband. In fact, she continued for two more years in ministry to the very people who killed him.

Don't let bitterness gain a foothold in your life. Seek God's help for an unforgiving heart. Search out any bitterness and failure to forgive, turn it over to your heavenly Father, and choose to forgive. You will be glad you did.

If you forgive men their trespasses,
your heavenly Father will also forgive you.
But if you do not forgive men their trespasses,
neither will your Father forgive your trespasses.
MATTHEW 6:14-15

Dealing with Sin

Lord, You are too pure to look upon sin.
Therefore, as Your Word says, if I harbor any wickedness
in my heart, You will not hear my prayers.
How can I ever even consider sinning when
I know it leads to severed communication
with You, the only One who loves me
unconditionally and knows what is best for me?
Please forgive me for the things I have failed to do.
And forgive me for what I have been doing that
displeases You. Help me keep and nurture a heart
that is constantly seeking Your forgiveness
so I please you and am assured
You are hearing my prayers.

Amen.

As a believer in Jesus Christ, you have an amazing privilege: You have a direct line of communication with the God of the universe through prayer. It doesn't matter where you are in the world. Unlike your cell phone, there are no dead zones, no roaming charges, and no dropped calls. The apostle Paul described the privilege and opportunity to pray in this way: "Be anxious for nothing, but in everything by prayer and supplication, with thanksgiving, let your requests be made known to God" (Philippians 4:6).

When you read Psalm 66:18—"If I regard wickedness in my heart, the Lord will not hear"—you have to ask yourself, "Why am I tolerating any sin in my life?" Sin not only blocks your communication with God, it also affects your daily walk with Him, your fellowship with Him. Your relationships with family and everyone you come in contact with are also hampered. You no longer exhibit love, joy, peace, patience, kindness, goodness, faithfulness, gentleness, and self-control, the fruit of Christlike character. Instead, you exhibit what the Bible refers to as "works of the flesh," which are awful things like strife, jealousy, outbursts of anger, disputes, envy, and a lot of other horrible actions (Galatians 5:19-23).

Quickly make a U-turn! Refuse to go down the road of sin. Confess your sin so you are "led by the Spirit" and enjoy sweet fellowship with God and the people in your life. Your relationship with God and His work in you is too important to allow sin to have a place in your life.

It is only deliberate, willful sin
that has not been confessed and forgiven
that makes us feel that God has forsaken us,
for that sin causes Him to hide His face from us.
ALAN REDPATH

Priorities

Thank You, God, that You are a God of order.
As I enter Your presence, I come seeking Your direction
for this new day. Father, my life is being pulled
in so many different directions. I don't know what to do.
I am immobilized in fear and dread that I will
spend my day in ways that might seem right and good
but, at the end of the day, will be of little value for
Your kingdom and for fulfilling my responsibilities
as a woman. Please give me wisdom just for today to
live my life in priority order—with You first, Lord.

Amen.

Do you ever feel like the person who got on a horse and tried to ride off in all directions at the same time? If you are like most women, whether single or married, you have lots of events, situations, people, and crises that can easily fill your every waking hour. You run like crazy all day and fall into bed physically consumed. But then, if you are truly honest (and you didn't immediately fall into an exhausted sleep), you might be brave enough to ask yourself, "What did I actually accomplish today that was truly significant, worthwhile, and had eternal value?" You probably did some good things, but could your

good things have been better things and—what's most important—the best things?

Having right priorities is the key to order, and that begins with
prayer. If you really want to know what God wants for your life,
you must take the first step and simply ask Him. Ask for His
direction and His will through prayer. Prayer shows your depen-
dence on God, and through prayer God gives you direction. As
Proverbs says, "Trust in the LORD with all your heart, and lean
not on your own understanding; in all your ways acknowledge
Him, and He shall direct your paths" (3:5-6). To be a Christian
who does not pray is like being a ship without a rudder.

Do you know what's best for your day? Your life? Set aside your
personal desires, and seek God's direction through prayer. Pray
each day as Jesus prayed: "Your will be done" (Matthew 26:42).
Ask God "What is Your will for me...just for today?"

...to love the LORD your God, to walk in all His ways,
to keep His commandments, to hold fast to Him,
and to serve Him with all your heart and with all your soul.

JOSHUA 22:5

Decision Making

Dear Father above, the greatest gift You have showered upon me came when You graciously chose to save my soul. I praise You that I will one day have personal fellowship and an eternal inheritance with You in heaven! But until then I must seek Your wisdom and counsel for the decisions I make each new day. My prayer is that I will live this day— today—in the fullness of joy as I seek to make the choices and decisions that will honor You. Thank You that I can discover Your will through prayer and Your Word. And thank You for Your promise to guide me into all truth. I know that as I daily choose to do Your will, You will lead me step by step on the path of life.

Amen.

Life requires that you make decisions, and there are many levels of decisions to be made. Some decisions are simple, like which breakfast cereal you will eat this morning. Other decisions are a little more complex, like which computer or phone to purchase. Still other decisions become even more serious, like buying a car or a home. Then there are the decisions about whether to homeschool your children or not, whether to change churches or not, whether to undergo chemotherapy or not. If you had to make very many of these serious decisions on your own, it could create a tremendous amount of stress and anxiety.

But praise God, He has not left you without help! He's given you the avenue of prayer—a direct line to Him. James 1:5 says it simply: "If any of you lacks wisdom, let him ask of God, who gives to all liberally and without reproach, and it will be given to him." He's also given you His Word as "a lamp to [your] feet and a light to [your] path" (Psalm 119:105) to show you His way. And God has given you other Christians to give you guidance and counsel. Don't be afraid to ask for help and advice. Ask as many people as you want, people who are knowledgeable, people you respect, people who will give you God's wisdom. And if you are married, ask your husband first. With these resources and God's guidance, you can make your decisions with greater confidence.

Delight yourself also in the LORD,
and He shall give you the desires of your heart.
Commit your way to the LORD, trust also in Him,
and He shall bring it to pass.

PSALM 37:4-5

Blessings

God of all blessings, I thank You that
You have blessed me with every spiritual blessing
through my relationship with Jesus Christ.
Because of His death on my behalf, I can experience
all the benefits of knowing You, Father,
because I have been adopted into Your heavenly family.
I bless Your name that I can now experience
Your forgiveness, and your Spirit's presence and power.
By Your Spirit I have the power to joyfully do Your will.
Thank You for these present blessings that
I can enjoy as I look forward to the future blessings
of living forever in Your presence.

Amen.

The Bible is abundantly clear that in Jesus Christ you are "blessed...with every spiritual blessing in the heavenly places in Christ" (Ephesians 1:3). These are spiritual blessings that you can experience both now and eternally. You have God's eternal blessings to look forward to, but until then, how can you experience God's blessing today?

In one word: obedience. In the Old Testament God had Moses physically place half of the Israelites on each of two opposing mountains to symbolically represent two opposing decisions.

Those who would choose obedience would be blessed, but those who would choose to disobey would be cursed (Deuteronomy 27:11–28:14). In the New Testament, Jesus defined obedience as an act of love when He said, "He who has My commandments and keeps them, it is he who loves Me. And he who loves Me will be loved by My Father, and I will love him and manifest Myself to him" (John 14:21).

Just as those in the Old Testament who disobeyed God did not experience God's blessings, neither should we expect God's blessings when we disobey. We choose to have our day and life blessed by God when we choose to be obedient to His will. How can you discover God's will? In five words: Read your Bible and pray. These two choices will bless you, and you will be a blessing to others.

> *Blessed is the man who walks*
> *not in the counsel of the ungodly,*
> *nor stands in the path of sinners,*
> *nor sits in the seat of the scornful;*
> *but his delight is in the law of the LORD,*
> *and in His law he meditates day and night...*
> *and whatever he does shall prosper.*
>
> PSALM 1:1-3

Open My Eyes

Lord of all beauty, how is it that I can look
but not see? I look at nature and fail to see
Your creative hand. I look at my circumstances and
fail to see Your hand of blessing. I look at my church
and fail to see where I can serve. I look at the people
around me and fail to see their need for a Savior.
I look at my heart and fail to see my selfishness.
I am blind and don't realize it! Please, Lord,
open my eyes that I may truly see the wonders of
the world around me—the world You have created.
Open my eyes that I may be enlightened
with the knowledge of who You are.

Amen.

The Old Testament has an encouraging story about the great prophet Elisha and his servant. While they were sleeping, their enemy's army surrounded the city. The next morning the servant looked out the window and exclaimed in fright: "Alas, my master! What shall we do?" What did Elisha answer? "Do not fear, for those who are with us are more than those who are with them" (2 Kings 6:16). Then Elisha prayed, "Lord...open his eyes that he may see." The passage continues: "Then the Lord opened the eyes of the young man, and he saw." Amazingly, the servant originally saw only the enemy! But after Elisha prayed, he saw the scene as Elisha did—"And behold, the mountain was full of horses and chariots of fire all around Elisha" (2 Kings 6:15-17).

Like this young man, you may tend to see only the enemy, the bad, the impossible. It's true that in the world you are surrounded by evil and hopelessness, and it would be easy to become fearful and lose hope. But the psalmist has the answer to our shortsightedness, which we can nurture daily. Pray, "Open my eyes, that I may see wondrous things from Your law" (Psalm 119:18).

The reason for poor spiritual eyesight is that we forget to look at life through the lens of Scripture. With God's Word as your lens, you can have complete confidence in God.

Do not be afraid.
Stand still, and see the salvation of the LORD,
which He will accomplish for you today.
EXODUS 14:13

Answered Prayer

Eternal Father, You are the One true God.
You are the only One in the world who hears and
answers prayer. Today, I confess my sin. I know that
You hear me in my distress and will answer my prayers
according to Your perfect will. Lord, hear my prayer
and my heart. Show me the way to handle some
heavy issues I am facing today. All praise be to You.

Amen.

Communication is a natural function in any healthy relationship, whether it is in marriage, the family unit, the church, or in the business world. And communication is especially important when it comes to your relationship with God. If you are His child, then prayer is the way you talk to your Father in heaven. But because God does not respond audibly, some people are convinced that God does not hear their prayers. Others think God isn't listening, or that He has chosen not to hear our prayers.

We can learn a lot from David about prayer and faith. David was confident that God would hear him and that God would answer his prayers. How could David have this level of confidence? David himself gives us the answer: He wrote in Psalm 4:3, "I know that the LORD has set apart for Himself him who is godly; the LORD will hear when I call to Him." God is a holy God and "of purer eyes than to behold evil, and cannot look on wickedness" (Habakkuk 1:13). The key to answered prayer is making sure we are faithful and devoted to God and obeying His Word. God is not looking for perfection before He responds to our prayers, but He is looking for a repentant and a humble heart. This is how you are to approach God with your petitions and prayers. Then you can say with confidence along with David, "The LORD will hear when I call to Him" (Psalm 4:3). Now read what David prayed next:

Stand before the LORD in awe, and do not sin against him.
Lie quietly on your bed in silent meditation.
Put your trust in the Lord,
and offer him pleasing sacrifices.

PSALM 4:4-5 TLB

Change

Life is full of changes—the beginning of life, death, career changes, marriages, health issues, the beginning and ending of friendships—changes both good and bad. Change is to be expected, but many times it is a surprise when it happens. Nothing stays the same from one day to the next—and at times, from one minute to the next! Unfortunately, we don't know what problem or crisis is lurking around the next corner!

Yes, life is full of uncertainties, but one thing you can count on with certainty is that your loving Father in heaven does not change. The psalmist knew this very well when he wrote, "You, O Lord, shall endure forever, and the remembrance of Your name to all generations." He concluded his psalm with these truths: "You are the same, and Your years will have no end" (Psalm 102:12,27).

If you are a believer—a child of God through Jesus Christ, His Son—no matter what happens to you, God's love, justice, wisdom, mercy, and grace will always be available to you, to comfort you, strengthen you, and hold you up. And as you read your Bible, you will read again and again that God's involvement in your life will always be good and helpful. The Bible gives you this promise of God's consistent goodness: "Every good gift and every perfect gift is from above, and comes down from the Father of lights, with whom there is no variation or shadow of turning" (James 1:17). In any of your changing situations, you can be assured that God will never change. And He will always be consistent in His character. He is the source of everything good, and everything He does is good. You can always count on God! Once again, God never changes.

> *Whatever the attributes of God were*
> *before the universe was called into existence,*
> *they are precisely the same now,*
> *and will remain so forever.*
>
> A.W. PINK

Praying for Your Children

*Your Word, Father, says if any will call upon You,
You will answer. Thank You for the privilege of
crying out to You on my behalf and for others,
especially my children. I come before You now, Lord,
as the only One who can make a difference in their lives.
You are the only One who can change their hearts.
The only One who can save their souls.
I am approaching Your throne of grace, begging you to
work a spiritual transformation in each of my children.
And help me, Father, to do my part to
"bring them up in the training and
admonition of the Lord"
(Ephesians 6:4).*

Amen.

They say a woman's work is never done, and that is especially true for mothers. From the day little ones are born, and right on through those joyous toddler years, the struggles of the teen years, and on into adulthood, a mom keeps busy—superbusy! But if we as mothers are not careful, we let the worldly cares of raising children interfere with the biggest care of all—the spiritual life of our children. In fact, the spiritual battle in and for each child rages their entire life, which means moms must intercede in prayer for each child's life and soul. Intercession for your children is not a sprint, but a marathon.

Praying for your children is to be relentless. Jesus gave an example of this in His story of a widow who came before a judge repeatedly about a personal concern. Finally, the judge gave her what she asked for, thinking, "Because this widow troubles me I will avenge her, lest by her continual coming she weary me" (Luke 18:5). Jesus praised this widow for her persistence, and she provides you with a model for continuing relentlessly to persist in prayer for your children as long as you have enough breath to pray.

Present your child to God, and present your case, your petition, your pleas to Him. Do it over and over, again and again. Pour out your heart to Him. Keep on coming before God Almighty. Keep on asking, seeking, and knocking, knowing that God alone is your greatest hope for your children. Do all you can and give your all. Pray without ceasing!

The prayer of a righteous person
is powerful and effective.
JAMES 5:16 NIV

Hope

*God, You gave hope to Noah and to
all generations when You promised You would not
destroy the world again with rain, giving Your people a
promise and a hope. I pray to recall Your promise so
I will not lose heart or be anxious or downcast.
God, You are my everlasting hope, and today I am
holding on to the hope of Your goodness with
every bit of strength I have. Your mercy is a sanctuary
that I can run to at any time. I praise You now
with my whole heart for the hope I have in You.*

Amen.

It's been said that a man can live for 40 days without food, five minutes without air, but not one minute without hope. Yet God has given us the rainbow to offer us hope and to symbolize His promise, saying, "The rainbow shall be seen in the cloud; and I will remember My covenant which is between Me and you and every living creature" (Genesis 9:14-15). As you face your uncertain future, hope is exactly what you need—hope that only God can give. You can definitely hope and count on God's continued goodness. Psalm 23:6 exudes hope, stating, "Surely goodness and mercy shall follow me all the days of my life." And what is that goodness? It is all of the attributes of God together.

Are you carrying a big burden right now? Whether it's a sick child, a lost job, an aging parent, or a teenager out of control, God knows right where you are and exactly what you need. Rest in this wonderful insight from Psalm 100:5: "The LORD is good; His mercy is everlasting, and His truth endures to all generations." This psalm is one of many in God's Word that are filled with hope and can encourage and strengthen your faith and trust in God. God alone can give you strength for today and bright hope for tomorrow.

Whenever you need God's strength for managing your day, rush to Him and His promises. God will be there. And the truths of His Word will be there. No matter how dark your day or your future looks, hold tightly to the hope of the promise of God's continual goodness and mercy. As the psalmist declared:

> *You are my hiding place and my shield;*
> *I hope in Your word.*
> PSALM 119:114

About the Author

Elizabeth George is a CBA and ECPA bestselling author of more than 100 books and Bible studies (more than 12 million sold). As a writer and speaker, her passion is to teach the Bible in a way that changes women's lives. For information about Elizabeth's books and to sign up for her newsletter and blogs, please contact Elizabeth at:

www.ElizabethGeorge.com

Books by Elizabeth George

- 15 Verses to Pray for Your Husband
- Beautiful in God's Eyes
- Breaking the Worry Habit…Forever
- Finding God's Path Through Your Trials
- Following God with All Your Heart
- The Heart of a Woman Who Prays
- Life Management for Busy Women
- Loving God with All Your Mind
- Loving God with All Your Mind DVD and Workbook
- A Mom After God's Own Heart
- A Mom After God's Own Heart Devotional
- Moments of Grace for a Woman's Heart
- One-Minute Inspirations for Women
- One Minute with the Women of the Bible
- Prayers for a Woman's Heart
- Proverbs for a Woman's Day
- Quiet Confidence for a Woman's Heart
- Raising a Daughter After God's Own Heart
- The Remarkable Women of the Bible
- Small Changes for a Better Life
- Walking with the Women of the Bible
- A Wife After God's Own Heart
- A Woman After God's Own Heart®
- A Woman After God's Own Heart®— Daily Devotional
- A Woman's Daily Walk with God
- A Woman's Guide to Making Right Choices

- A Woman's High Calling
- A Woman's Walk with God
- A Woman Who Reflects the Heart of Jesus

Books for Young Women

- Beautiful in God's Eyes for Young Women
- A Young Woman After God's Own Heart
- A Young Woman After God's Own Heart— A Devotional
- A Young Woman Who Reflects the Heart of Jesus
- A Young Woman's Guide to Discovering Her Bible
- A Young Woman's Guide to Making Right Choices
- A Young Woman's Guide to Prayer
- A Young Woman's Walk with God

Books for Girls

- A Girl After God's Own Heart
- A Girl After God's Own Heart Devotional
- A Girl's Guide to Discovering Her Bible
- A Girl's Guide to Making Really Good Choices
- You Always Have a Friend in Jesus for Girls

Children's Books

- Through the Bible One Rhyme at a Time
- God's Wisdom for Little Girls
- A Little Girl After God's Own Heart